n

Wholeness

Hidden Wholeness

An African American Spirituality
for Individuals and Communities

MICHAEL I. N. DASH
JONATHAN JACKSON
STEPHEN C. RASOR

United Church Press
Cleveland, Ohio

United Church Press, Cleveland, Ohio 44115

Printed in the United States of America on acid-free paper

02 01 00 99 98 97   5 4 3 2 1

Library of Congress Cataloging-in-Publication Data

Dash, Michael I. N.
    Hidden wholeness : an African American spirituality for individuals and communities / Michael I. N. Dash, Jonathan Jackson, Stephen C. Rasor.
        p.   cm.
    Includes bibliographical references.
    ISBN 0–8298–1164–8 (pbk. : alk. paper)
    1. Afro Americans—Religion. 2. Spirituality—United States.
I. Jackson, Jonathan, 1930–   . II. Rasor, Stephen Charles.
III. Title.
BR563.N4D37 1997
248'.089'96073—dc21   97–3691
                                                          CIP

Contents

Preface

It has been said that "the church exists to serve the world and the seminary the church." Whether this is true or not is debatable. What may be less in question is the present condition of the world. The world appears to be void of any universal religious meaning, certainly not an embracing spiritual wholeness. The world has become disenchanted and the church paralyzed in its attempt to influence needed change. The seminary appears to take its primary cues from educational perspectives more secular in nature, and thereby experiences itself as confounded when attempting to address any loss of religious meaning in the world. Hence, church and seminary leadership feel frustrated. Both sense that something is missing but are not certain of just what it is.

We risk claiming that we have some idea concerning what is missing. We suggest that a hidden wholeness, connecting individuals and communities, is absent. The wholeness is hidden, because otherwise it would become common and mundane. It is hidden so that we will not and cannot make an idol of it. God hides the Divine self so that we do not misuse God. What is hidden can be known if we have the right eyes for seeing. That which is hidden is real and visible. Mystics see the hidden, because their eyes are cleansed. William Blake said, "If we had clean eyes we could see the world in a drop of water."

We contend that there is a yearning for wholeness, indicative of a spiritual hunger in our world. Any search to address this desire for wholeness is only authentic as it is willing to affirm and include the contribution that can be made by the African American experience. This book is an invitation to join in the search for and the discovery of this wholeness, which the whole human family can experience as we all acknowledge that we participate in a suffering and broken world.

A hidden wholeness guides the interconnecting themes of this book: spirituality, theological education, ministry, and liberation. It is our hope that discovering this hidden wholeness may offer significant direction for the work of seminaries and energize the mission and ministry of the church.

Spirituality is an important topic for many groups of people today. When we use the word, we suggest a unique and liberating dynamic. Spirituality involves individuals and communities in a tripartite and cyclical process: a liberating encounter, a liberating reflection, and a liberating action. Spirituality is more than a personal experience. It is a communal quest and adventure to discover wholeness only to be realized in community. It is certainly more than something we feel. It is something that involves us in new kinds of behavior, saying "no" to whatever limits full participation in community. It is a spirituality that demands creative integration, contemplation, and engagement. The route to holiness (wholeness) Dag Hammarskjöld wrote, "necessarily passes through the world of action."[1]

We teach in an interdenominational setting that prepares women and men for ministry. We ourselves are Protestant clergy. We have served as local parish pastors and presently teach from a practical theological perspective. We write out of a passionate commitment for the plight of theological education and for ministerial training in general. We want to share our feelings and ideas about the role of spirituality in the training of ministers and the role of pastors functioning in the church. It is an invitation and challenge to rigorous pursuits of mind as well as earnest and deepened devotion to life in the Spirit.

We desire for this book to produce three primary outcomes. First, we offer you, the reader, and others in your faith community the opportunity to explore the unique contributions of an African and African American spirituality. For some of you, this will generate new insights; for others, a reaffirmation of something you have already experienced. Second, we invite you and others to reflect on a type of liberating spirituality that integrates faith and action—in the context of church and world. Finally, we hope through this book to challenge the larger Christian community. The challenge we issue calls all of us to participation in this liberating spirituality, through life in church and community—in this one world.

This is a liberating spirituality that African and African American peoples have embraced and continue to embrace as a means of survival and hope. It is a spirituality that has enabled them to break through the historic layers of degradation, injustice, and oppression—and yet still celebrate life! This book proposes to illustrate how some African American traditions can serve not as a means to supplant the European models of spirituality, but rather as prophetic and reconciling agents. It is a book for everyone who yearns to experience that wholeness which can only enrich all in the human family.

The book comprises five chapters. In the first, which introduces our assumptions about spirituality, we will clarify our model, suggesting that spirituality involves us in a liberating encounter, liberating reflection, and liberating action. The second chapter will explore the origin of African American spirituality in response to Western societal existence. The third chapter will highlight the sociological reality or African journey of an oppressed people in the larger world and Western society. Chapter 4 will give a more communal and institutional grounding for African Americans' experience of suffering and pain. Finally, chapter 5 suggests that the journey continues for all of us—people of color and otherwise. It challenges us to join together, following the invitation of God, in establishing a world and society more akin to God's original purpose.

Our book includes the tales of real persons. They are not intended to define the spirituality of which we write, nor should they be interpreted as characterizing the African American experience. We cannot speak of one distinctive, homogeneous experience or single cultural identity of any people, not even among African Americans. The tales are of individuals who struggle to be human, to live out and express their humanity. We trust that these tales will challenge and inspire you as together we explore this spirituality of hidden wholeness.

The text provides exercises in spirituality, found in appendix 1. Appendix 2 provides suggestions for using the questions for reflection and action which appear at the end of each chapter. As a final word, appendix 3 encourages reflection on the "Million Man March." The rest is up to you. Actually, the rest is in the hands of the Liberated One who calls us out of ourselves and into the world of a liberated reality.

One of our fundamental beliefs is that contemporary men and women are fragmented, self-centered, and pulled in many directions because they lack a unifying purpose. They do not base their lives on a central core of existence. The longing for wholeness is not something we can manufacture within ourselves. It must come from God, who challenges us to respond to the Divine presence and the Divine call. Our response must be authentic. The wholeness that we yearn for is the Christ, who makes God real for us. It is this life in God, that we affirm God offers us still.

Acknowledgments

We appreciate the many persons in our ITC family who provided support and services, in various ways and on several occasions, while we were engaged in this project. We think particularly of those colleagues in our departments who put up with crabby handwriting and numerous requests for retyping of revisions. In this regard, special thanks are due Helen D. Bell, Melody Lewis, Jacquelyn B. Hurston, Martha Lewis, and the late and lamented Betty R. Butler.

We would not have been able to bring this manuscript to publication without the tireless devotion of Reta L. Bigham. She labored over the years as our copyeditor. Her selfless commitment is only matched by her knowledge, expertise, and professionalism.

For reading the work, for giving us interviews, and assisting in other ways, we thank Noel Erskine, Jim Fowler, and Luther Smith of Candler School of Theology; and Cynthia Hale and Kathy Sage. We appreciate the help and talent of Will Studstill, who designed the diagrams used in the text. From our own school, we express our gratitude to all our colleagues, and in particular, Cassandra R. Baker, Jacquelyn Grant, Frank Johnson, Carolyn L. McCrary, the late Thomas J. Pugh, Ndugu T'Ofori-Atta, and Calvin S. Morris, our academic dean. President Costen continuously gave encouragement along the way by making constant reference to our work in a sense of realized eschatology: There was no doubt that it *would* come to life.

In the fall semester of 1992 and spring semester of 1996, we team-taught a course on spirituality, exploring some of our ideas and perspectives. The participation was spirited and enthusiastic. We are indebted to members of those classes who seized the opportunity not only to critique our efforts but to share their own stories. We have included some of those stories in our work.

For financial assistance, we thank the members of our school's Faculty Status, Tenure, and Welfare Committee. Accepting a grant from that committee obliged us to vindicate their faith in our ability to bring this work to a successful conclusion. We trust that our work honors our entire community.

Finally, each of us is grateful to members of our immediate families, whose love and devotion we especially value: Linda, Ginneh, Michelle, and Nathaniel Dash; Alberta Jackson Davis and Jennifer C. Jackson; and Susan and Joshua Rasor. Their endurance of disruptions to family life along the way has increased our respect, honor, and love for them.

Narratives of Encounter, Reflection, and Action

Before advancing an understanding of African American spirituality (chapter 1), we need to share, briefly, our individual and unique spiritual stories. We have arrived at this point in our common life originating from different contexts. Our journeys have not been the same, but our desired destination appears to be complementary. We bring these experiences to the task of writing this book and advocating a spiritual wholeness.

Any discussion of spirituality should start with a note of personal engagement. Yet it must also begin in an openness to the presence of God. Only a commitment to a deeper understanding and exploration of life in the Spirit avails for continuing daily existence. Without this perspective, the integrity of any spiritual discussion would be suspect.

My Personal Journey: Michael I. N. Dash

My earliest recollections of encounters with God were in Sunday school, which was at three o'clock in the afternoon and a little less than a mile away. In a hot tropical country, we were aware of the heat rising off the asphalt pavement and the concrete sidewalk; but, looking back now, it did not seem to be important then. Our teachers—particularly two whom I recall most vividly—walked greater distances than we did to get to the school, and they always seemed to be already there when we arrived.

Miss Benjamin and Miss Clarke are two teachers I remember very well. Neither of them ever married. Miss Benjamin was a fairly tall woman, "thin-boned" as we used to say; Miss Clarke was short and pleasingly plump. When I returned home for a visit after being out of seminary for several years, I found that Miss Benjamin had died. Miss Clarke had aged considerably and become a much smaller and frailer figure. These kindly women exuded a warm, maternal love for the children under their care. They assured us by word and in deed that "Jesus loves the little children," expressing tender affections with hugs and consolations, carefully patting away tears of anxiety.

At home our mother told us the stories of Jesus, which we loved to hear.

> . . . how the children stood round his knee,
> . . . scenes by the wayside, tales of the sea. . . .[1]

Her constant love and affection followed us over the years. All of her seven children except my sister June migrated to the United States or Canada. Mother never traveled, even when one of my brothers offered to bring her to Canada for his wedding. She reluctantly permitted our sister, who predeceased her by three years, to go.

And when I went through the pain of divorce, she constantly wrote to assure me that she was praying for "her son." It was a simple faith in the faithfulness of God: that God would take care of her sons—even Michael—in that distant land. That faith was what I recalled when I celebrated her life and preached at her funeral.

My father, blessed be his memory, taught me Latin (at least some words) long before I went to high school: "Mens sana in corpore sano (a healthy mind in a healthy body)." He was so disciplined and tried to inculcate (that was one of his words—a good word) in us the rigors to which he subjected himself. He rose early and engaged in breathing exercises, inhaling "God's fresh air," as he would say. When he was younger, he used to run—maybe it was jogging, long before it became fashionable for health enthusiasts. In later years, he took to walking. He constantly impressed on us the connection between mind and body, laying on that Latin quote to enforce his point. "Health is the first wealth," wrote Ralph Waldo Emerson, the New England philosopher. My father read Emerson and bequeathed to me a collection of his essays.

It was also in the early morning that my father called us to prayer. We would all kneel around our parents' bed and talk to God about our life—its struggles, its joys, its concerns. These last always included relatives and friends about whom we were especially anxious. It was a good God who sustained us and was present in all our lives.

The church and church services held a significant place in our family life. Near our house lived the Huntley family, in which there were even more children than in ours. We developed a deep relationship with the Huntleys. On Sunday evenings, they would walk to our house and call us out; then we would join them, walking to church in one parade. When the two fathers met, Mr. Huntley invariably said to my father, "Donald, "happy is the man who has his quiver full" (Ps. 127:5). (He used the verse from a psalm to describe the number of children in the two families.) When we arrived at the Trinity Methodist Church in Georgetown, we filled one long pew.

My pastor was the sainted Errol Stanley Montrose Pilgrim. He was a humble, selfless, and self-effacing man. He said, "I never aspire to any position in the ministry," and he exemplified this humility in his life. This remark has helped to shape my attitude to my vocation over the years. It was during his tenure that I went to seminary. Two other associates who came to work with Mr. Pilgrim also encouraged me along the way. They loaned books and started me on the way by giving me the opportunity to share in liturgy. My first public reading of scripture was from Isaiah 53. The saints at Trinity thereafter affirmed a call to ministry, and I claimed I knew. Mr. Pilgrim had retired to his native Barbados by the time I was ordained. I wrote to tell him about it and to thank him for his influence on my growth in Jesus Christ. Always with sage counsel, plainly stated, he wrote to me giving his blessing. I still cherish that letter today.

Then when I became a local preacher, the Department of the British Conference of the Methodist Church sent me a letter (a personalized form letter). It reminded me and others who received it, as it constantly reminds me even today, of the need to "explore the measureless tracks of the spiritual life only to be experienced through the adventurous experiments of prayer and Bible study." Spirituality has to do with relationship to God. If it means anything at all, spirituality means life with God in Jesus Christ. It begins with an initial encounter and is sustained through a continuing relationship with God in the discipline of daily life. It is further sustained by our willingness to be open and sensitive to the movement of the Spirit in our lives. It means seeking to live within God's will. God's will always challenges and calls us to love through our relationship to others, through offering our whole selves—body, mind and spirit—to God. Perhaps some understanding of our willingness to live in this way finds expression in a hymn which calls us to prayer:

> Dismiss me not Thy service, Lord,
> But train me for Thy will;
> For even I, in fields so broad,
> Some duties may fulfill;
> And I will ask for no reward,
> Except to serve Thee still.[2]

My Personal Journey: Jonathan Jackson

My father died when I was two years old, and I do not remember him. I remember my stepfather, who died about twenty years ago. It may be that for all of my life I have been looking for my real father. From my childhood on, I have had occasions to meet father guides who have been father surrogates. I have always had a special interest in persons who represent for me the ideal of "the hero"— mentally, emotionally, spiritually, and physically exceptional. Such figures I have always thought of as "the Venerable Sage." Somehow I always have wanted to be a wise old man who is a teacher and mentor to the young. Even now, I am a great reader of biography and have sought to interview and meet the exceptional people of our time.

I wanted to be different, not necessarily high in worldly honors, but I wanted to achieve and know it myself. I did not care if anyone else knew it. I have usually felt that God was with me, surrounding me and protecting me, but sometimes I have slipped from that belief.

When I entered the first grade I could read, but because I could not recite the alphabet I was placed in a retarded or slow class. The classroom was divided into smart rows and "lazy" rows; the smart students met in the morning, and the "lazy" students met in the afternoon. I was in the "lazy" row in the afternoon. One day, when I was five or six, the teacher heard me reading and was fascinated. She picked me up and carried me to the principal's office and said, "Listen to this, you won't believe it." The principal heard me read, and I was immediately transferred to the smart row in the morning session. This incident influenced me greatly, adding to my feeling— true or false—that I was different.

Later I was influenced by one of my great-aunts, who was a griot. Many people from the community would come to her for healing and counsel. I watched my aunt and admired her: Although she could not read or write her name, she had a kind of intuitive wisdom.

In my first year of college, I had a different kind of experience: I flunked out. While I was out of school for a year, one of my father guides helped me to weather the storm. After returning to college, I made the honor roll until I graduated. Later I enrolled in seminary. Another guide—who had taught me in Sunday school, college, and seminary—made me strive for excellence.

My studies at Boston University were the high point of my early life. I met a very pretty and intelligent young lady, and later we were married. From that relationship came a beautiful daughter. Although this relationship became broken after twenty years, it was a tremendous spiritual experience for me. From it I have seen vistas of myself open up that have made God more and more meaningful to me. I believe the challenges of my life have been beneficial to me as a minister teaching theological students to follow their paths in seminary training.

Another part of my spiritual growth occurred during my sabbatical at ITC. Sabbaticals, spirituality, and theological education are multidimensional in scope. I discovered many definitions of spirituality during my sabbatical leave, but the one I liked best was by Anthony de Mello, the Jesuit priest. He said that spirituality was waking from sleep—not just a physical sleep but sleep as a lack of awareness. De Mello identified sleep as the nature of the human condition, citing the example of a mother who came to awaken her son for school. She said, "Wake up, son, it's time to go to school." The son replied, "No, Mother, I am not going to school today." The mother asked why, whereupon the son said, "The students can't stand me, and the faculty members don't like me either." His mother responded, "But son, I can think of three better reasons why you ought to go to school today. First it's your obligation to attend; second, you are forty-three years old; and third, you are the principal!"

During my sabbatical, I was aroused from sleep, like this young man, in a multidimensional way. Many people think that taking a sabbatical will provide peace and calm, along with the chance to do library research, to think, and to conduct interviews without difficulties, problems, or pain. But this is a myth, I found. Sabbaticals are multidimensional. While I was on my sabbatical, my mother developed an illness and could not walk. Since she lives alone and I am her only offspring, I had to look after her completely, working my travels, interviews, retreats, and reading around her care. At the same time, I had dear friends who were hospitalized and needed my ministry.

Despite these complications, along with other sometimes painful incidents, my sabbatical did afford me moments of space and contemplation with which to view my entire life and see it in perspective. So my sabbatical was not a unidimensional experience of peace and quiet, but rather a multifaceted one of conflict and quiet. The mystics might say that it was taken "Amidst the Dark Desert Experiences of Life."

> Lead, kindly light, amid the encircling gloom,
> Lead thou me on!
> The night is dark, and I am far from home;
> Lead thou me on!
> Keep thou my feet, I do not ask to see the distant scene;
> one step enough for me.[3]

My Personal Journey: Stephen C. Rasor

God, the church, and my mother were interwoven in my early years. I remember returning from church camp and announcing to my parents that I had been called by God to go into the Methodist ministry. My mother responded, with great authority, that she already knew that was the case!

It was in college and finally seminary that I began the process of separating these influencing factors. My exposure to professors who seemed to integrate personal faith and acts of social justice helped me begin a new awareness of religiosity and particularly of spirituality. It was and is a spirituality that attempts to consolidate God's presence in faith (being) and God's presence in social behavior (doing).

In May 1970 several African American students were randomly killed in Jackson, Mississippi. I was a senior at Millsaps College, a small United Methodist liberal arts college in the area. I participated in a protest march and prayer vigil in response to that vicious and racist slaughter of young life. Admittedly, my involvement was trivial compared to so many others, both at Millsaps and Jackson State University (site of the murders), before and after that event, but it was a spiritual turning point for me—in so many ways.

My first senior pastorate in rural Georgia, from 1974 to 1978, was another significant transforming period. My bishop assigned me to preach the gospel of Christ Jesus, twice a week in this humble setting. Early on I became acutely aware of my spiritual emptiness. I was supposedly the spiritual leader of this small congregation, and yet I was keenly conscious of my deep-seated hunger for God. I turned to the spiritual disciplines of scriptural reflection, meditation, and prayer to discover a deeper source of existence.

When I came to the Interdenominational Theological Center in 1985, I discovered a world I had not known. It was and is a seminary setting that allows its students to articulate both their suffering *and* their joy. They cry out against an oppressive society with a voice of anguish and pain. Too often their voice has been ignored by much of North America. It is an environment that produces a holistic spirituality that calls for justice and prayer.

I am fortunate in that God has allowed me to participate in this theological setting. I have discovered a God of the oppressed, who both condemns and liberates. I have experienced many things as a part of this faculty, some of which are quite painful and yet ultimately redemptive.

I am in my middle forties, and in too many ways, am "middle way" spiritually. I have seen, heard, and experienced—as a child, college/seminary student, pastor, and seminary professor—some significant things that have awakened my soul. And yet I feel so utterly immature in the faith. I have witnessed a spiritual dimension, one that connects social activity and spiritual formation. However, I really have only just started. My pilgrimage is in its earliest stages. I am barely on the road. God has been kind to pull me along thus far. I do look forward to what is coming next.

The first verse of the hymn "Awake, O Sleeper" is consistent with my experience of the spiritual journey:

Awake, O sleeper, rise from death,
and Christ shall give you light;
so learn his love, its length and breadth,
its fullness, depth and height.[4]

1

"Breaking through the Pavement"
Our Exploration into Spirituality

You have seen trees growing out of sheer rock; or roots, finding no soil below or being unable to penetrate the rocky substance of the earth, spread themselves, fan shape, on the surface, sending their tendrils into every crevice and cranny where hidden moisture and soil fragments accumulate. You have seen human beings with their bodies reduced to mere skeletons and all the vestiges of health wiped out—yet for interminable periods they continue breathing, as if to breathe were life.[1]

Howard Thurman, in his reflection on "The Will to Live," describes an event in his life that helped him experience existence at a deeper level. While walking down an Atlanta, Georgia, street, Thurman observed a tree that had broken through the concrete pavement. The pavement could not contain the tree's desire to live. In breaking through, the tree exemplified the determination to live. The ability to discern profound truth in the midst of everyday life experiences was one of Howard Thurman's many gifts.

Thurman was a multidimensional person who lived on all levels of existence—physical, emotional, and spiritual. Describing his attributes is like constructing a bridge. The bridge, to be effective, must reach both sides, or the traveler will fall.

A poem we read once might relate to Thurman at this point:

Not "how did [one] die?"
But "how did [one] live?"
Not "what did [one] gain?"
But "what did [one] give?"
These are the units to measure the worth of a [person],
as a [person], regardless of birth.[2]

Thurman was an acknowledged preacher, educator, mystic, pastor, and humanitarian. Perhaps Vincent Harding captures "this God-intoxicated" man best when he wrote about Thurman in the introduction to *For The Inward Journey*. Harding observed that Howard Thurman was a person who was constantly moving toward the source of all human life and truth via the concrete beauty and terror of the black experience in the United States.[3]

While one of us knew Howard Thurman personally, all three of us knew Charles Presberry. "Presberry," as we called him, was one of our students. He recently died; cancer claimed him from this side of life. We remembered and celebrated his life on several occasions in our seminary setting. Students, staff, and faculty members gave rich testimony to the many ways in which Presberry touched our lives.

Presberry's life, illustrated in the words of Howard Thurman, suggests one of the reasons we have written this book. Our dear friend Presberry lived his life in ways similar to the meaning expressed by Thurman in "The Will to Live."

First, he was an older student, and many questioned his purpose for attending seminary. Presberry, an engaging conversationalist, freely communicated that he was determined not to let his age keep him from growing theologically. Like Thurman's tree imagery, Presberry pushed beyond the assumed wisdom that seminary training and theological knowledge were only for the young. He, like other African American students, did not accept the "paved-over" limits of society, race, or age restrictions. He had the "will to live" and continue his education. God was "not finished with him yet."

Second, Presberry, like most of us, experienced the heights and depths of emotions as he lived his many years. Whether he was facing a cancerous segregated society or the cancer in his own body,

Presberry consistently broke through the pavement of his despair. He learned early how to express himself and share his deepest feelings. He felt deep emotional discord at times; he was incredibly buoyant at other times. During his life, Presberry appeared to be one who would not allow the limiting concrete of existence to arrest his discovery of the depth and height of living.

Third, Presberry faced death with courage and assurance. While our society has devised ever-so-creative ways to deny the facts of aging and death, he modeled for us a "will to live" in and beyond death. We are certain that he is observing us today from somewhere on the other side—with a smile on his face. He would tell us not to deny death but to break through its reality and overcome it. This is the essence of the greater Christian story and one we hold as we train men and women for ministry, like Charles Presberry.

Remembering Presberry made us think of life, and the spirit that he showed through his life. This book is about spirituality, which is often understood as a technique of meditation. Our exploration of the subject proposes that spirituality is broader and beyond technique. It has to do with the spirit that one exhibits in life through relationship with God and others. This sense of being in touch with who one is arises from a liberating encounter with God who, in Jesus Christ, frees us from bondage—from all kinds of restrictions. Jesus challenges us to serious reflection of his life, and empowers us through his resurrected life "to break through the pavement" in the search for wholeness, this freedom to be truly human. It is a story that we have heard, it is the story we will tell, and a story we must help to make. Our discovery of this fundamental "wide and deep urgency," in the words of Howard Thurman, is the foremost impulse in this work.

The Liberating Aspects of Spirituality

"Spirituality" is a common term but used in a variety of ways. There is a spirituality of persons or individuals. There can also be a spirituality of groups or organizations. It can be used to describe an attitude or way of life, like a spirituality of consumerism or even a spirituality of hedonism. It can be Christian, drawing on multiple, and at times different, biblical images. It may not be exclusively Christian and can thus describe a Buddhist, Hindu, Muslim, or Jewish spirituality. It must always be seen within the culture, society, and religious orientation from which it originates. Its context often influences its usage. Hence, "spirituality" varies significantly in current communication.

In general, our notion of spirituality suggests that all people have some sort of spirituality: All people hold fast to something. We order our lives based on some fundamental essence. At the core of our being, we love someone or something deeply. We live life, in part, grounded in that "prior love."

We experience love and learn how to love within a social setting: the family, the neighborhood, school, church and wider society. Therefore, our spirituality may be described as being personally experienced, but in fact it is a reality created within the community of others. We are spiritual beings but within a larger spiritual context. We are "we" and not simply an "I" as we develop a deeper spirituality. True spirituality can never ignore what happens to our selves in our communities. Herein lies a recurring challenge to us as humans: It is to recognize and affirm our interdependence that we *are* one another's keepers.

In the Judeo-Christian tradition we claim a "prior love" that is connected with or to the Spirit of God. We make the faith claim that God takes the initiative in creation and breathed into humankind a living spirit—in Hebrew, *nephesh*. In the person of Jesus, we experience the incarnate holy God and thus the revealed depth of God's love. Our "prior love" is a response to our being loved. Hence, our spirituality is a state of being grounded in the Spirit of God and God's love expressed in Jesus the Christ.

God, us (individuals and communities), the world, the church, the seminary—all are locations of exploration in the life of the Spirit. The Spirit needs a home with large spaces in order to be free to move, to grow, and to expand in our lives. It is then that we become open to discovering the hidden wholeness.

In the late 1980s, the World Council of Churches assembled a group of people to explore "spiritual formation in theological education." Several understandings came out of this ecumenical study of spirituality and theological training. "Spirituality," as they described it, "points to life in the spirit, and Spiritual Formation refers to being nourished and sustained in such a life." Spirituality has something to do with the character of the truly spiritual life, and spiritual formation, how that life can be sustained and nourished.[4]

The participants involved in this worldwide study of spirituality, argued that our

> present crisis of spirituality arises from a fundamental dysfunctioning in the lives of people—in relation to God, to . . . human beings and to their own selves. God has been dethroned from the hearts and minds of people. The God whom Jesus Christ revealed to us is no longer conceived as one who controls the forces of history. Humankind itself, and other gods, have taken God's place.[5]

The persons gathered at the meeting represented different denominations and communities, but most were Christians. Thus, their concept of spirituality was unapologetically Christian in tone: "All true Christian spiritualities help those who follow Christ to walk and live in God's presence with body, mind and soul, in the midst of the sufferings and struggles of this world."[6]

We affirm many of the ideas expressed by this ecumenical study process. Christian spirituality does involve those of us who claim God in Jesus, in the whole of life—both its joy and suffering. We are not removed from the real world by our spirituality; rather, we are thrust the more in it. We experience the pain, suffering, and anguish of human existence, along with some of its joyous happenings. God invites us to join God in God's world. God is there; we must give ourselves to the task of active participation *there*, even with all of its consequences.

We contend that spirituality for the individual, as well as groups of persons, can result in a liberating experience. As the following diagram illustrates, this liberating experience has three dynamic and interconnecting components. At one point is a liberating encounter, followed by a liberating reflection. In turn, we can experience a liberating action. This encounter, reflection, and action can penetrate and transform our individual and collective activity. We encounter God, because God intends that encounter. God is already active in the world, and we encounter God's presence. To be encountered by God is a liberating event, for God is the giver and sustainer of life. God, as Matthew Fox explains, is like an "underground river," which cannot be stopped. "God's energy will not be aborted," it flows into the lives of persons and communities because God is at the center of all existence. God's creative energy is at the heart of our spiritual encounter.[7]

Following that encounter, we experience a liberating reflection. That reflection can take many forms often associated with the so-called spiritual disciplines of prayer, meditation, scripture reading, storytelling, and worship. These disciplines provide a basis for the development of long-term spiritual formation. As we encounter God, the ground of our being, we are urged, impelled to do something in response. This in our Christian tradition often involves spiritually forming events, disciplines of the Spirit—prayer, sharing, worship, and service.

Finally, the encounter with God and the initial response to God

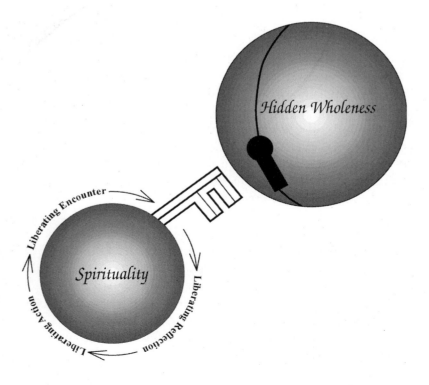

arise out of God's initiative. The God whom we seek finds us. To be found of God is to experience a liberating encounter, whatever reflective form that encounter may take, which pushes us to a liberating action. This action is one that drives us outward and into the lives of others in the world in continual acts of self-giving. It is freeing when, as a result of the encounter/reflection, we are required to join God in God's liberating action in the social institutions and personal lives of God's people. Our spirituality is truly a liberating and whole one when we are compelled by the Creator and the creative energy of spiritual reflection to participate with God in the life-giving acts of justice and peace in God's world.

Thus, spirituality can result in liberation: a liberating encounter, a liberating reflection and a liberating action. Ours is a God who initiates this liberation from within the center of our being (the individual) and in the midst of our everyday activity (the collective) in the world. This liberating spirituality, we contend, is the key to our discovery of a hidden wholeness.

Unfortunately, there are Christian men and women who assume that spirituality and liberation are not connected in any meaningful way. Some would argue that they are opposites. This is a "great fallacy," according to Robert McAfee Brown. While Judaism never attempted to divide life into separate spheres, others have certainly done so. Brown points to an earlier dominating Greek worldview, certain Christian "desert fathers," key medieval religious figures, and the "two-tier reality" notions of the Protestant Reformation as significant historical resources for this great fallacy. The fallacy suggests that our existence can be divided into two rather distinct parts: sacred-secular, faith-works, church-world, soul-body, spirit-flesh, saint-sinner, prayer-politics, etc. So many people accept this dualistic worldview that it is challenging to hear anything else.[8]

The problem this creates is a concept of spirituality that is, for the most part, otherworldly, individualistic, and elitist, and it rarely fosters social change. It reinforces a presupposition that liberation, on the other hand, is this-worldly, communally oriented, and solely focused on social transformation. This is a false understanding of both of these terms.

Brown argues for a redefinition of spirituality and liberation. Spirituality includes all of life; it is more holistic, not a separate reality. Spirituality involves a simultaneous commitment to persons and God. It has to do fundamentally with following Jesus, as well as claiming him as Savior.[9] Liberation calls us away from unjust social systems and into a world where we actively participate in the creation of a just society. Liberation involves us in responsible action, both individually and in community. Liberation frees us from a condemnation of sin and guilt and propels us into a grace-filled existence.[10]

Gustavo Gutiérrez calls this a spirituality of liberation, one that undergirds a liberation theology. This theology is grounded in an authentic encounter with God. This prophetic Latin American theologian in no way accepts some artificial divide between liberation and spirituality. *Conversion* to the Christian life is a prerequisite for solidarity with the poor. God's *grace* becomes the basis for social action. *Joy* points to victory over suffering and death. *Spiritual "childhood"* is a requirement, for all of us, if we are really committed to the poor among us. And *community*, Gutiérrez reminds us, draws Christian men and women "out of solitude" and into connectedness. We are a people in search of God in community.[11]

We claim a kind of spirituality that is holistic and dynamic. For us, it involves whole communities and whole persons. Spirituality involves us in a liberating encounter, a liberating reflection, and a liberating action. And yet the starting point for that liberating experience may originate in action. As we give ourselves to full participation in God's world, we often encounter God. We allow ourselves time to reflect on that encounter through prayer, worship, or the telling of our story. In other instances, the encounter may occur in solitude but quickly compels us to participate in community. Thus, our basic understanding of spirituality is dynamic and cyclical in nature: It suggests a reality that is whole and embracing, not divided and alienated.

There are too many destructive ideologies in contemporary life that enslave rather than liberate us. Our institutionalization and individual manifestations of racism abound still. We are creative but exacting in our sexist acts and institutional form. We are a society severely divided by class. The wholeness of God's creation remains hidden as long as we allow these ways of seeing and explaining the world (ideology) to dominate.

As a nation, our history of the annihilation of American Indians; enslavement, exploitation, and attempted genocide of Africans; as well as our various imperialistic and militaristic exploits in the world, suppresses the wholeness and potential completeness of the God-created order.

Our spirituality must be such that it drives us to build relationships. It must reunite us with our Creator. It is not some kind of personal piety that has little to do with others and the world. It has everything to do with our relationships with and among peoples in this one world. Other women and men, other persons representing different ethnicities and classes are in this world with us. We are "in this" world together. We were so created to be in community, one with another. It is a destructive idea to see one's spirituality as something that we only do or experience individually. We are blind to the wholeness of the created order if we assume that spirituality has nothing to do with the social, economic, and political life of our neighbor—both next door and across the globe.

Moses encountered God in his life and the lives of the Israelites. Their enslavement contradicted his encounter and reflection on the ways of God for humankind. God led Moses to lead God's people out of bondage and into a liberated existence.

Christ Jesus, whom we claim as God and Savior, offered his life for us all. Jesus' life, death, and resurrection are the most compelling and liberating acts of God in our history. God gave the Divine Self for all of humankind. A text, that we might in some ways know too well, argues for this liberating action on behalf of our Creator God:

> For God so loved the world that [God] gave [God's] only [Child], so that everyone who believes in [God] may not perish but may have eternal life. Indeed, God did not send [that Child] into the world to condemn the world, but in order that the world might be saved through [the Child]. (John 3:16)

Our reaffirmation of the Christian story places us in that story. Our individual stories must be seen in light of that larger story. Spirituality, for us, is a liberating process that grounds us in one primary source. The discovery or rediscovery of this source of existence enables us to affirm our particularities, but seen in an unusually larger frame of reference.

There is a hidden wholeness available to us. It often remains "hidden" because we choose to move away from God, enslave others and thus ourselves, and pretend that spirituality is only a small and private segment of our being.

Like the Athenians in Paul's day, we choose to worship an array of idols. Our idols may not be quite the same, but they do exist: racism, sexism, economic exploitation, materialism, environmental suicide, etc. We need to hear again Paul's words to those gathered at Athens:

> The God who made the world and everything in it, is [the God] who is [Sovereign] of heaven and earth, does not live in shrines (or ideologies) made by human hands, nor is . . . served by human hands, as though [God] needed anything, since [God] . . . gives to all mortals life and breath and all things. From one ancestor [God] made all nations to inhabit the whole earth, and [God] allotted the times of their existence and the boundaries of the places where they would live, so they would search for God and perhaps grope for . . . and find [God]—though indeed [God] is not far from each one of us. For "In [God] we live and move and have our being"; as even some of your poets have said, "For we too are [God's] offspring." (Acts 17:24–28)

The text directs our attention to the fact that a wholeness does exist—one that we have available to us, one that is as close to us as our very breath *(nephesh)*. We can choose to participate in a transforming kind of spirituality that reveals that wholeness. To do so may mean for some of us that we look for new resources in African and African American spirituality. Or for others of us, it simply means coming home.

Slave Religion and Spirituality

Africans, transported to the New World through the Middle Passage, brought with them a certain set of religious beliefs. They

brought also a memory, individual and collective, of certain structures of religious behavior and practice. Africans were not stripped
of their culture during slavery. There were vigorous efforts to sup-
press and deny it. Over time, African slaves came to accept and
adopt the Europeans' religion, to shape and fashion it to their own
peculiar needs.

Aunt Jessie's mother was born into slavery. And Aunt Jessie remembers and recalls a legacy her mother left behind. It was that of
living in the presence of Jesus. Jesus was real to Aunt Jessie, as he
was to her mother. She claimed not so much that prayer was no
longer necessary, but that prayer was a state of "feeling the spirit,"
of being in Jesus. Jesus on whom she could call , in affliction was always present to her. In every situation of distress, struggle, challenge
or triumph, happiness, joy—Jesus was with her. She agreed for Jesus to change her name and knew that he would be with her as she
sought "to live a humble life."

Slave religion developed as a living response and a peculiar creation that reflected the experiences and conditions Africans knew in
the American context. This is the heritage of African American religion that relates the way in which a people encountered Aunt
Jessie's Jesus "down in the Lonesome Valley" and in "de wilderness." In their oppression, slaves found it natural to identify with
the sufferings of Jesus—who, in the spirituals, was depicted as an
ever-present and intimate friend. Slaves identified with this Jesus and
interpreted his crucifixion both as tragedy and hope. He was their
companion on their journey, someone who understood and walked
with them in their sufferings and their joy. Thus they came to view
God's presence in the Spirit as an empowering presence that enabled
them to respond to the reality of their contradictory experiences.
The encounter with Jesus was liberating. Their meditation and reflection on that encounter, in the midst of the troubles they saw in
bondage and their response through the Spirit, were for them as for
their descendants—a way to liberation and freedom.

This book discusses religion in general and spirituality in particular from an African and African American perspective. It is a special spirituality because it grows out of the experience of a unique
people of color who have encountered a God who sustains and lib-

erates. Spirituality expressed in African and African American culture offers the larger Western society a fresh and enriching spirituality unexperienced by far too many European Americans.

The suffering, pain, and daily anguish of most African Americans and many African peoples is beyond the existential comprehension of a significant number of European Americans. The joy and ability to celebrate life, expressed by many people of African heritage in response to their long history of suffering, *are* more than most outsiders can begin to understand. And yet this unique spirituality, breaking through the historic layers of degradation, injustice, and oppression in the black community, provides a discovery or rediscovery of spirituality—possibly for the whole human family. We argue that that which has been hidden or submerged in the larger Western culture is that which is most needed. It offers a promise and hope for all humankind.

African American Religiosity

Fundamentally, everyday existence raises a prior compelling question. It is the question of meaning and purpose in the face of our many problems and crises of meaning. Clifford Geertz defines religion as a cultural symbolic system that empowers the human community to deal with chaos and threatening problems of human existence. Geertz believes that our many sacred symbols (objects, acts, events, qualities, or relations) enable us to deal with bewilderment, suffering, and injustice. Our analytical, emotional, and moral questions of meaning motivate us to explain anomalous events, making suffering sufferable and enabling us to cope with the limits of our moral insight.[12]

African American religiosity, at its core, models this comprehensive understanding of religion. Black religion in America, originating from West Africa, the Caribbean, and the United States, represents a unique black sacred cosmos. Its African heritage, Caribbean adaptation, and North American response to white Christianity gives it a special character. "Black religion," according to Gayraud Wilmore, "began in Africa, was mixed with European Christianity in the Caribbean and in Latin America, and was further molded by, and recoiled *from*, American evangelical Protestantism on the slave plantation of the South and among the tiny communities of free blacks in the North."[13] It comes into being in the midst of severe pain and suffering, dating from the period of slavery and colonization to the present. Black religion is unique to black people. It is a religiosity that enabled an oppressed people to cope with their suffering, thus making suffering somewhat sufferable. It has provided and provides today a black sacred worldview—a larger frame of reference for explaining the unexplainable. It offers hope in the midst of an unjust society. It represents "shared pain, shared history, and shared hope of liberation"[14] for African Americans in this country. It points to a deeper spiritual reality.

The holy encounter of Africans and African Americans with the Holy One, their reflective response and action to that encounter, formulated in the midst of overwhelming suffering, forged a spirituality that can only be described as liberating. This dynamic liberating essence, which we call "spirituality," enables many black people to both claim their sorrow and express their joy. The power to go down and come back up, to "come out of the wilderness" and offer the world a spirituality so expansive points to the power of God. In reaction to evil ways and systems, God created in the souls of black folk an existential awareness of Godself—one that obviously begins in the heart of God. Our intent, in writing this book, is to share that story with others, and invite their participation in the discovery of wholeness.

Black religion, and the form it has taken in the African American religious experience, illustrate for us the kind of spirituality we are advancing in this text. Spirituality and social transformation are key interconnected parts of the African American sacred cosmos. It has been authoritatively argued that the primary vocation of the black church is one that interrelates spirituality and social transformation. Similar to our perspective, spirituality involves a liberating experience. The African American church has never attempted to separate these realities.

> What we call the black religious tradition nurtures and promotes both spirituality and militancy for social change in varying and complex ways; that both in the official actions of the

denominations and in the black church as a mass-based, folk institution, religion and politics are inseparable; and further, that spirituality and social transformation are not only two sides of the same coin, but are so interpenetrated that the black religionist cannot rest comfortably without both.[15]

Nor can we "rest comfortably" unless we present a kind of spirituality that promotes a liberating encounter, liberating reflection, and a liberating action.

We have written this book together. We refuse to explore spirituality without expressing it in a collective sense. Our individual understandings are shaped by our mutual life together. Spirituality is not an "I" reality. It encompasses the "we." We offer our experience to you, the reader.

We are theological educators, teaching in an interdenominational setting among mostly African and African American persons. Interdenominational Theological Center (ITC), where we teach, is a consortium of six Protestant seminaries. While all three of us are Protestant ministers, one of us teaches Christian education; one field education; and the other, sociology of religion. Our backgrounds include an African American experience, an African-Caribbean heritage, and an European American perspective. We all share the common concern for discerning and practicing a spirituality that is grounded in a black liberating experience, as we endeavor to educate persons for ministry and extend ministry ourselves.

We wholeheartedly invite you to join us on this journey. We trust that you will discover or rediscover a sense of your own spirituality as you engage this text. Beyond our words, we hope that you, too, will encounter God, reflect on God's meaning for you and others, and dedicate yourself to significant action in your faith community and world.

The reading of this book can enhance the spirituality process that engulfs you and your community. If you allow it, and more importantly the Spirit of God, to liberate your heart, mind, and hands, we all will be the better.

After you explore the following questions for reflection and action, we invite you to consider or reconsider, in chapter 2, the heritage and journey of African and African American spirituality.

Questions for Reflection and Action

1. What are some ways in which your sense of who God is and who you are in relationship to God is affecting your life with others?

2. Examine carefully the diagram presented in chapter 1. Identify its strengths and weaknesses for you as you seek to understand and engage in the view of spirituality that it depicts.

3. Select two or three spirituals and reflect on ways in which they speak to your life situation as well as to persons you know or have known.

4. How do you understand the "spiritual life" or "life in the spirit?" What are some of the fundamental ideas in that understanding?

5. Look at Mark 9:2–13. What does it mean today for you and for a group of Christians to "listen" to Christ (v. 7)?

2

"No Other Tale to Tell"
Our Heritage and Journey

For, while the tale of how we suffer, and how we are delighted, and how we may triumph is never new, it must always be heard. There isn't any other tale to tell, it's the only light we've got in all this darkness.[1]

In "Sonny's Blues," a long short story, and *Just above My Head*, a lengthy novel in five books, James Baldwin explores the terrifying journey of the possibilities and failures of love. He employs the blues-gospel narrative as a technique for achieving his objective. On another level, the statement at the beginning of this chapter may also describe the turbulent journey of African Americans in this society. It is the story of the struggle of being black and poor; of experiencing the depths and the heights, the blues moan and the gospel shout, dirge and hymn, death and life.

Baldwin knows and asserts "that whoever cannot tell himself the truth about his past is trapped in it, is immobilized in the prison of his undiscovered self. This is also true of nations."[2] He also reminds us that "accepting one's past—one's history—is how to use it."[3] In *Just above My Head*, he continues to explore the themes of learning how to use one's individual and group past and discovering that personal suffering is a bridge to others.

In both "Sonny's Blues" and *Just above My Head*—which is, in some ways, an extended version of that story—the blues-gospel narrative is used as an art form to tell his story. Baldwin succeeds in integrating gospel music into his prose as he expands on his thematic concerns. The blues, in its function, form, and impact, conveys the nexus between individual and community identity. The first-person narrator of "Sonny's Blues" tells the story of Sonny, his younger brother, from his youth to his arrest on drug charges and ultimately his release after treatment. The narrator's personal pain, stemming from the death of his younger daughter, moves him to contact Sonny. Sonny's piano playing provides a way for the older brother/narrator/reflector to discover the meaning of their separate but interrelated lives and to be reconciled with his younger brother.

Baldwin's statement of the "tale that African Americans have to tell" was written nearly three decades ago. Many contemporary African American writers and artists (using varying media—paintings, sculpture, and music in many forms) are self-confidently telling their story in all its complexity and with all its contradictions. It is this continuing story that is the source of their spirituality.

The Changing Canon in Religion and the Issue of Spirituality

There is an ongoing and earnest quest by African American scholars to understand and affirm the influence on and the contribution of the African heritage to our common life in the United States. A spate of books by African American scholars, within the last ten years, has challenged existing canons.[4] A basic contention is that the canon (on studies of religion in America) in Charles Long's words, "has rendered the (religious) reality of non-Europeans to a state of invisibility";[5] there is not even a notation about them in any significant monograph on American religion. Lincoln and Mamiya, in their long-awaited and monumental study, make the claim, "that to exclude it (African American religion) runs the risk of a seriously distorted picture of what American religion is like."[6] We posit that as African Americans, self-affirmation carries within it its own authenticity. It has value, it enables a people unabashedly to get on with their life in spite of a stamp of inauthenticity being placed on it by others.

An exploration of African Americans' experience cannot be fragmented. There is for them, as for Africans, an interrelatedness in all of life—work, play, and worship. It is difficult, for instance, to discuss African Americans' religion or art or literature and not recognize this interconnection. Thus, a reflection on the changing canon must include examination of these connections.

Henry Louis Gates has illustrated how black artists, using different media, and black writers have sought to redefine their personhood and their humanity. This redefinition has made it necessary for "each black person . . . to dig himself or herself out from under the codified racist debris of centuries of representation of blackness as absence, as nothingness, as deformity and depravity."[7]

Even though Gates is specifically discussing the work of artists, we contend that he is describing reality in the whole of the African American experience. African American culture, Gates proposes, "has been a model of multiculturalism and plurality."[8] What he says about the culture includes the religious experience and spirituality: that "this cultural impulse . . . represents the very best hope for us, collectively, to forge a new and vital, common American culture in the twenty-first century."[9] We also believe that an appreciation of African American spirituality can contribute to "hidden wholeness."

Different and peculiar are not and should not be ascriptions of negation. It is the distinctiveness, uniqueness that we wish to examine, state, claim, reclaim, and offer as contribution and challenge for enrichment in our common journey in the United States and among humanity. Perhaps what needs to be heard and acknowledged is that "our history and our present being are a mirror of all the manifold experiences of America. What we want, what we represent, what we endure is what America *is*."[10]

Spirituality is becoming increasingly prominent in discussions of the Christian religious experience. As we indicated in chapter 1, the World Council of Churches, in 1987, held a consultation on the subject in Scotland. A basic and working definition proposed in that consultation was that "Spirituality points to life in the spirit, and Spiritual Formation refers to being nourished and sustained in such a life."[11]

Howard Thurman stated that in his work he sought to "utilize the raw materials of daily experience as the time and the place of the encounter with God."[12] It is this understanding of spirituality, as has been experienced by African peoples and African Americans, that guides perspectives we explore in this work.

Kofi Asare Opoku reminds us of this pervasive role of religion or its "absorbing character" in Africa, where the whole of life is wrapped up in religion. A particular notion of reality that runs through African culture is the complementarity of relationship between the spiritual and the material. One may even propose that spirituality is reality. "The African concept of [a hu]man, for example, is that he [or she] is made up of body and spirit, but by far the greater part of [a hu]man is made up of spirit."[13]

Indeed, this idea of the spiritual includes the ancestral spirits, who play a prominent role in the religion:

> Death . . . does not end life; it is an extension of life. There is firm belief that a community of the dead exists alongside the community of the living and . . . there is a mutually beneficial partnership between them. Human society, therefore, has an extra human or supernatural dimension to it because the dead remain part of it. The dead, the living and the yet unborn form an unbroken family.[14]

Such spirituality reflects a wholeness in life that affects the way we reflect and respond to our existential realities.

Books and articles suggesting various kinds of spiritualities have come from major publishing houses in the United States. One publisher's representative speaks of "spirituality" as an overworked subject. "Not another book on spirituality," he pleaded in a discussion with us, "except from your (ethnic) perspective." We seek to respond to that and more. We argue that the search for wholeness in our society and in our world is only authentic as it is willing to affirm that African American culture is not "exclusively a thing apart, separate from the whole, having no influence on the shape and shaping of American culture." As African Americans, we need *ourselves* to understand our culture, its roots, and its heritage. Most importantly, we need to recognize, affirm, reclaim, and celebrate the heritage that is ours. It will counter this nihilistic threat under which we stand. For "the genius of our black foremothers and forefathers was to ward off the nihilistic threat, to equip black folk with cultural armor to beat back the demons of hopelessness, meaninglessness, and lovelessness."[15] We need equally to understand how our culture is affecting and can impact the dominant culture.

North American representatives to that 1987 WCC consultation met before and after that gathering and developed some key documents by way of response. Their work has heightened interest in spiritualities. We seek to respond to some real concerns about theological education and spiritual formation as suggested by the following questions: How can we strengthen the relationship between spirituality and the kind of teaching that is done within the theological seminary? How can we make this relevant to the North American context? How can we bring together European Americans and African Americans in the United States to develop a spirituality that is meaningful to all of us? We wish to explore and suggest that what we offer at ITC, out of an African American experience, can bridge the gap that seems to exist between the theological seminary and understandings and practices of spirituality.

Heritage, Tradition, and Spirituality

A clichéd idea holds that every human being is a product of his or her past. This is historically as well as psychologically true. It is no less true spiritually. There is a connection between God's dealings with each person and each person's past.

The biblical writers affirm this connection in many places. Israel knew this fact as she experienced her history: "for I . . . your God am a jealous God, punishing children for the iniquity of parents, to the third and fourth generation of those who reject me, but showing steadfast love to the thousandth generation of those who love me and keep my commandments" (Deut. 5:9–10). One's genealogy is important, but one is not merely a product of one's past. One's creation is of God with a unique individuality. God made human beings in God's image (Gen. 1:27). Yet we are not divided personalities—that is to say, beings with bodies which are products of the past and souls of God's creation. Such bifurcation is a reflection of Western thinking. The Greeks thought of human beings as mortal bodies with immortal souls. Hebrew thought was more integral in its outlook. "The Hebrew idea of the personality" (in a sentence that H. Wheeler Robinson made famous a long time ago) "is an animated body, and not an incarcerated soul."[16] Human beings are total personalities: body, mind, and spirit. The body is an integral part of the human being. We are not a single origin of two different and separate halves. Our wholeness derives from two sources—earth and heaven—flowing into our beings.

When the Bible speaks of human beings as made in God's image, the suggestion is that it is the image of reflection, as the image of one's face in a mirror. It is not a stamped image, like the image of a dead president on a coin. We have the capability of reflecting God. That is what we are meant to do. Human beings as bodies are products of our past. Human beings equally, as souls, are reflections of God's image.

A genuine spirituality both seeks to discover this oneness and give expression to this hidden wholeness. Spirituality is not something that one strives to attain. It is to be lived in daily life. It is to be "manifested in the desire not just to refrain from offending the ancestors, but more especially to attempt positively to remember them and make them part of your life."[17]

The tale that Africans, and subsequently African Americans, tell is of a people who understand and perceive this sense of unity of personality. Life for the African is one integral whole. All aspects of life are joined in an inseparable link. The religious dimension pervades the culture; African culture is a religious culture. This sense of the religious is also present in African peoples in the diaspora and no less evident in African Americans.

Spirituality begins for Africans before they are born, and spirituality never ends. Both the search for and the discovery of hidden wholeness are ongoing. To search is to discern where we might work for and make manifest the community that God wills for all human beings. The spirituality on which we are reflecting, one emerging from the African and African American heritage, fosters life in community, and always calls attention to what happens to us—all of us—among ourselves in community.

African Spirituality: Shapes and Continuities

There is no disagreement that the African heritage persists within the cultural expressions of Africans in the diaspora. This is evident in the religious beliefs and practices of their slave descendants in

America. Theories of the extent of the influence will perhaps continue to be debated. E. Franklin Frazier, Robert Park, and G. R. Wilson shared the view that the religion of Africa disappeared from the consciousness of the American slave.

Melville J. Herskovits was chief among others who held an opposite view. He contended what common sense confirms—that religion was not removed from life but deeply integrated in slaves' day-to-day existence. Thus, no compelling case could be made for complete eradication. Slave religion, we propose, was a continuity of African ancestral religion. In contact with European Christianity in American colonial and slave society, African American religion became an inventiveness within a tradition. It reflects a transformation that took place on American soil. We will briefly examine the shapes and continuities, new creations and forms that emerged in the religious experience of the Africans who were transported to America.

A most confirming factor for us is the way in which religion informs every aspect of African American life. Slave religion in brush arbors; the "invisible institution"; storefronts; New Orleans jazz; the black Muslims: Elijah Muhammad, Malcolm X, and Louis Farrakhan; Jesse Jackson and Martin Luther King Jr.; the culture of hip-hop and the contemporary and popular rap culture; Michael Jackson and Michael Jordan—all evidence the seminal religious influences in the whole of life: work, play, and worship. Indeed, the spirituality of African Americans finds expression in all these diverse ways. Although many rocks may come from a single quarry, many varying elements comprise those rocks. Similarly, any attempt to describe African Americans or their spirituality in monolithic terms must necessarily be false.

Much of the literature on African American spirituality has tended to focus quite correctly on the contribution of African traditional religions. Mbiti reminds us that "we speak of African traditional religions in the plural because there are about one thousand African peoples (tribes), and each has its own religious system."[18] Several scholars, while not in total agreement with Mbiti's use of the plural, have written of African traditional religions as a source of African American spirituality.[19]

It must be noted that the Africans who came to these shores and the slave masters who themselves were immigrants were creating a whole new society, developing new cultural forms and practices. "Cultural change . . . is a process affecting one or both (or all) of the peoples in contact; this process is often analyzed in terms of the concepts, acculturation and assimilation."[20] If we accept that cultural change is continuous, then continuity from an African base is the best way to explain the evolution of African culture in North America. "It is not a pathological reaction to extreme social deprivation."[21] What is manifest, even in transformation, are those common and seminal elements in a core culture. African American spirituality reflects this process of transformation in North America.

In the traditional African heritage, spirituality began at birth and never ended. Learning about life and how life was to be lived were informally taught. Hospitality, kindness, duties of spouses, the behavior of children in public and private all formed part of one's development as a human being. Spirituality was not something for which one strove. It was lived in daily life. "Where genuine spirituality thrives, individualism and egoism should give way to communal values. We are one another's keepers."[22] This is often not the case today.

This is evident to a number of us who teach in theological seminaries, because even there we have not been immersed in a holistic liturgical movements as we should. There is a pervasively false notion, as one of our colleagues, Randall Bailey, persistently reminds us, that we know that we are spiritual when we trash intellect. Spirit and intellect are not disjunctive, but conjunctive. The Eurocentric influence of dualism (discussed in chapter 3) is so strong that this tendency to disjuncture is often exhibited in statement and in practice in our chapel experiences. Some preachers say: "They taught me Bultmann, Tillich, Greek, but . . . " or "As soon as I leave these halls, I will get back to Aunt Jane's stuff."

Mbiti tells an imaginary story that reflects, by contrast, an opposite perspective. An African spent nearly nine years in Europe studying theology, earning a coveted doctorate on some obscure theologian of the Middle Ages. When he steps off the plane on returning home, a crowd is there to greet him. (In Africa even though an achievement is individual, the degree belongs to the community. "We" have earned this doctorate.) In the midst of the jubilation,

there is a shriek. His older sister is taken ill. "She is demon possessed," they cry. He shouts back, "Bultmann has demythologized
demon possession."[23] It is a dilemma clamoring for attention and
resolution.

What we are trying to show is the importance of the African
worldview and African religions. They are all a part of an effort to
move away from the European dualism, discussed elsewhere, to a
kind of unified cosmology which we find in the African religions.
Africans believe in a Supreme Being, ancestors, sacrifice, spirits, ritual, drumming, chants, medicine people, and sorcerers. The whole
idea of life is that it is to be lived to the fullest. For the African, life
is one integral whole. There is an interrelationship among the several aspects of life: Social life, politics, economics, morality, spirituality all constitute the "stuff" of life. Human life and existence are
guided by religion as a motive principle. Much of this is also a part
of contemporary African American religion. If we are to make any
kind of contact, if we are to effect any kind of transformation in
churches struggling to integrate spirituality into theological education, it becomes possible as we recognize that in the roots of African
American spirituality there is a movement from dualism to a more
holistic worldview.

In a recent work, *The Spirituality of African Peoples*, Peter Paris
accepts that the great diversity of culture prohibits any generaliza-
tions about Africa. Further, even though vast differences are manifest in each cultural context, broad structural components can be
identified in the moral and religious thought of African peoples.
Paris seeks, in his work, "to demonstrate how that structural factor
which originated on the continent of Africa has survived in many
modified forms throughout the African diaspora."[24] Paris claims
that his understandings center on "integrally related and overlap-
ping dimensions of African cosmological and societal thought,"
which include:

1. the realm or spirit (inclusive of the Supreme Deity, the sub-
   divinities, the ancestral spirits), which is the source and preserver of all life
2. the realm of tribal or ethnic community which, in equilibrium with the realm of spirit, constitutes the paramount
   goal of human life

3. the realm of family, which in equilibrium with the realms of tribe and spirit, constitutes the principal guiding force for personal development, and
4. the individual person who strives to integrate the three realms in his or her soul.[25]

We commend Paris's work to our readers. In it, he achieves his objective of illustrating "how those understandings (of African cosmological and societal thought) fared under the conditions of North American slavery and the eventual formation of a syncretized cosmology comprising an amalgam of Christian and African elements."[26]

The shapes of African spirituality have emerged out of their complex cosmologies. These have helped persons in their sundry attempts to relate to and explain the realms of reality: spirit, history, and nature. Fundamental to a cosmology and consequently to spirituality is the understanding of God. The ideas of God as creator of the universe and human beings, transcendent of divine power, preserver of all life, and the final authority and arbiter in all matters are firmly entrenched in the religious beliefs of African peoples. As Paris asserts: "Africans in the diaspora were able to preserve the structural dimensions of their spirituality: belief in a spirit-filled cosmos and acceptance of moral obligation to build a community in harmony with all the various powers in the cosmos."[27] It is these trace elements and expressions that can be noted as continuities in the slave period of Africans in America and beyond, into the present day.

A true spirituality cannot be constructed or assembled. It has to be recognized in the daily life of people who seek together to make sense of their existence and find meaning in life for themselves as individuals and in their collective experiences. The continuity between African and African American spirituality can thus be illustrated.

We seek to show shapes and continuities by reference to a fascinating autobiography. It is *Of Water and the Spirit: Ritual, Magic and Initiation in the Life of an African Shaman*.[28] The writer, Malidoma Patrice Somé, reminds, according to one reviewer, that "we must learn to walk the 'braided' way and bridge different worlds without losing our ancestral roots and spiritual integrity."

So in several places, the heritage and the journey of African Americans can be noted. Shapes and continuities of their spirituality can be traced.

Africans in the diaspora, but no less so in the United States, continue to take children to view the dead in a coffin or casket. Somé is describing the several rituals relating to his grandfather's death and funeral.

> Before the burial, the grave must be *muul*, literally 'looked into,' a ceremony that allows a viewing of the final residence of the dead. This ritual is for children only. They get the opportunity to see what a grave is like, and to remember the last resting place of a person of status. For years afterward they will always be able to recall the name of the person whose grave they looked into, and this helps determine how much time has passed since then. For the Dagara, the child's memory works better than the adult's. If you trust something important to a child, he or she will keep it as long as he or she draws breath.[29]

Today, in the United States, we are almost forced to abandon our dead as soon as possible after the funeral at the grave site. The funeral director announces the end of the ceremony with the invitation to return to our cars. The ritual of staying until the last shovel full of dirt covered the grave are a distant memory. It must be noted, however, that in some islands in the Caribbean, this ritual persists. Persons sing hymns and encourage the gravediggers until a mound of earth stands to mark the grave, whereon wreaths are placed.

As Somé recalls and illustrates in his autobiography, funerals and burials include rituals that reflect mourning and celebration. Musicians, males and female separately, tell their tales of death and life, life and death, for "Death is life and life is death. The dead live while the living die. Living or dying we have joy."[30]

Many tales are told of the significance of music in the life of Africans and African Americans. In the cotton fields and plantations of the South, African Americans labored from sunup to sundown, singing as they worked. Participating in the singing and music making was not only a form of community experience, it also served to provide power for arduous labor. Indeed, music making helped to invite African Americans into a participatory group activity for a common purpose. And on the plantation, it helped to get the work done.

Singing and working, heavy work and creativity are expressions of the connectedness of life. They also confirm that for Africans and African Americans spirituality affects their whole life, whether at work or play or worship. "In order to combat the monotony of the labor, the women would sing genealogy songs, which were long enough to last the six hours it took to grind a bucket of millet."[31] Somé goes on to illustrate the connection between singing and working, labor and creativity. As he says of his mother, "without her improvisational singing, she might not have been able to sustain this monotonous work from noontime till dusk."[32]

How Africans understood God, community, family, and persons gave shape to their spirituality. These separate but interdependent dimensions of their cosmological and societal thought are reflected in continuities as expressed in the various forms of African American spirituality.

African American Spirituality: Sources and Conventions

African American spirituality has many sources and conventions. These several sources have been combined in the evolution of the African American church and the spirituality expressed within its institutions.

African Traditional Religions and African Culture

The fundamental sources of African American spirituality are African traditional religions and African culture. As Jamie Phelps asserts, " . . . the study of black spirituality probably begins with a look at the African worldview and African traditional religions."[33]

If we accept that basic premise, then we must continue to contend that spirituality, in its varied expressions, is inclusive of the whole of life for African Americans. There is the persistent carryover between Saturday night and Sunday morning, blues and spirituals. African Americans attempt to bring together polarities. In typical European versions of Christianity, sacred and secular are kept apart. In the African American experience, there is "the intersection of . . . two master stories—its 'mundane' story and its 'sacred' story."[34]

African and African American spiritualities eliminate the dichotomy, the dualism found in most European spiritualities. The sacred and the secular are overcome. Separateness of male and female is overcome. Social and political matters are overcome through a spirituality in which there is no division. The personal is overcome in the communal. This breaking up of the dualisms comes about at the deepest philosophical level. We might also describe it as the cosmological level. In Western philosophy it would be at the level of metaphysics and ontology. The African American believes that all is one. In many ways this is one of the main reasons that there is such a problem with theological education and spirituality in the West. The assumption of most Europeans is that life is bifurcated. That is where we start under the influence of the dominant culture. In starting from that particular perspective, all other difficulties ensue.

It is important to make these observations at this point in our discussion of sources and conventions of African American spirituality. For the expressions of the spirituality are unconfined to the church and its institutions. Yet the church and Christianity as sources have contributed significantly to the formation of a culture that continues to be pervaded by an intense religiosity.

In a very useful diagram illustrating the core elements of African American culture, Jacqueline Butler has built on the work of Wade Nobles. Those elements as reflected in that diagram explore "who we are," "what (and we would add, how) we know," "what we feel," and "what we do."[35] We would contend that the representations and configurations of those elements are to be found in all African Americans. For example, under the section, "Self-Identity" (who we are), the following are listed: extended self, interdependent, familial, spiritual, collective, communal, faith undergirds, contextually dependent, resilient, relationally creative. As we examine the conventions of African American spirituality many of these elements will be presented. This amalgam of symbols, ideas, and practices, drawn from a variety of sources, originates in African traditional religions.

Protestant and Evangelical Traditions

Albert Raboteau deals extensively with the contribution of Protestant and evangelical traditions as another source of African American spirituality.[36] These ideas convey a seminal notion that all humanity is *radically* equal before God, particularly in sinful equality. A standard sermon preached on the plantations was on the theme "Slaves, Obey Your Master." Many narratives are told about some slaves' response to the instructions that followed on that text. One such story is of Uncle Silas, who questioned: "Is God gonna free us slaves when we git to Heaven?" The white preacher offered the explanation: "Jesus says, 'come unto me ye who are free from sin an' I will give you salvation.' " Uncle Silas, undaunted, rebutted, "Gonna give us freedom 'long wid salvation?" The preacher continued, and Uncle Silas remained standing up front during the rest of the service.[37] Like so many others, slaves refused to accept the white people's notion of God that black people were to serve whites and *maybe* receive some "pie-in-the-sky" reward after death.

Both in North America and in the Caribbean, slaves were drawn to the preaching of Methodist, Baptist, Presbyterian, and Congregational clergy. In the Caribbean, the African slaves who heard the gospel rejected any attempts to spiritualize it. Their response was in a freedom-oriented faith. The notion of freedom was unconfined to salvation from sin, but rather it included life in all of its dimensions. The African American tale is of the pilgrimage of a people toward freedom. It is a quest for that transcendent and inclusive community in which the imperatives of freedom and justice are honored.

Civil Religion

A third source of African American spirituality is civil religion. As Robert Michael Franklin understands it, it is "this emerging overarching set of myths and beliefs that were defining America as a new nation; the notion that persons could experience radical re-birth in American culture."[38] African Americans continue to participate in the various traditions of American civil religion—the ceremonies, the observances, such as Thanksgiving, Memorial Day, and the Fourth of July. They have embraced and called into question the motto on our coins, "In God We Trust." Clergy have been functionaries, offering prayers at major public as well as private functions.

As Charles Long has observed, "The distinction between civil religion and church religion is not one that looms large for us."[39] Long goes on to suggest that it is no accident that black churches were, not unnaturally, the place where the civil rights struggle was carried out, because "it represented the black confrontation with an American myth that dehumanized the black person's being."[40] It also illustrated the interconnection between religion and culture in the African American experience. One expression of spirituality was the popularity of the song, "We Shall Overcome!" During the civil rights movement, it became not only a rallying call but a power for uniting persons who identified with and were committed to the struggle.

Roman Catholicism

Catholic popular piety, especially as was evident in Louisiana and Maryland, was an additional source of African American spirituality. Catholicism's liturgical structures suggested some parallels to features in African traditional religions. Slaves, as well as free blacks, found deep meaning in a piety centered on the Mass and devotion to the Blessed Virgin and the saints. Colorful vestments, sacred objects, candles, holy water, incense, and so on, are also some evidences of similarities. As in Brazil and Cuba, the Catholic church provided slaves opportunity for the organization of religious fraternities. These became for the slaves not only a mechanism for the preservation of African religion but also a supportive community.

The Atlantic slave trade, which transported Africans from West Africa to the Americas, also created during those two centuries "a new ethnic conglomerate; gradually a people of common identity emerged out of tribal groups as disparate in Africa as the Wolof in the northwest, the Yoruba and Ibo on the central coast, and the Angolans south of the Congo."[41]

Islam

It must be noted that *Islam* arrived in Senegambia on the African continent about the eleventh century. Widespread conversion to Islam did not occur until the late nineteenth century. Although the slave trade was legally terminated in 1808, trading continued far beyond that date. It is not unreasonable therefore to assume that African religion, as it was transmitted to the Americas, had been influenced by Islam. Some of the slaves transported to the Americas were already people of the book—the Koran. They were literate in their native tongue as well as Arabic. Perhaps this strong desire for literacy, to want to read and write, reflects such a heritage.

There is no agreement on the legitimacy of the present-day black Muslims as fully and properly representative of the major principles of Islam. It must be noted, however, that like Judaism and Christianity, Islam has afforded a prominent role to prophets. Muhammad is considered the special messenger of Allah (God) and the last prophet. So also, among the history of the black Muslim movement in America, Elijah Muhammad became the special messenger of Allah. "The African American role in Islam is best distinguished through the establishment of the black Muslims."[42]

Subsequent sects and variants of black Muslims were established including the Organization of African American Unity, led by Malcolm X after his visit to Mecca and his break from Elijah Muhammad. Other important groups to be noted are American Muslim Mission, led by Warith Dean Muhammad, and the Nation of Islam, led by the charismatic and continually controversial Louis Farrakhan. What we have said about the black church can be said about the Muslim religious experience: It is not monolithic. Islam, in its various religious beliefs and practices, was also a significant source of the emerging core culture of African American spirituality. Wherever the faith is practiced by whatever branch of Islam, there is placed upon devotees a demand for high ethical standards of behavior. There is a constant attempt to match belief with its expression in daily living.

Biblical Christianity

Biblical Christianity became a significant source of the spirituality of African Americans. It was the Bible that enabled our slave ancestors to learn to read and write. The slave preacher based his sermons on the Bible. The stories, the characters, and the images, both from the Old and New Testaments, informed not only preaching but praying and singing. Bible stories, ideas, and concepts were foundational to faith affirmations in the spirituals.

"The slave's Bible was constructed primarily from the books of Moses in the Old Testament and of Revelation in the New. All that lay between, even the life of Jesus, they rarely cared to read or hear."[43] Janice Hale goes on to state that stories of the life of Daniel, David, Joshua, Jonah, Moses, and Noah fed the imagination of the slave to make connections between their own experiences and those of the biblical characters.

Raboteau reminds us that "it is not surprising that the use to which slaveholders had put the Bible would lead some slaves to distinguish between their own experiential Christianity and the 'Bible Christianity' of their masters."[44] Christianity, as they observed it among their masters, was such that slaves were unwilling to embrace it. The slaves appropriated the message for themselves and translated it in terms of their own experience. The spirituals became a medium through which the slaves expressed characters, themes, and lessons of the Bible. That body of songs became a source of our slave ancestors' spirituality. It enabled them to survive the brutality of slavery and cherish hope that "trouble (wouldn't) last always."

Apocalypse

Theophus Smith explores the perspective of Apocalypse in "biblical formulations of black America" (the subtitle of his impressive work).[45] He contends that "attention to apocalyptic figuration is integral to a display of the full range and interests of African American conjurational spirituality."[46]

"Apocalypse" is the word that John, the author of the biblical book of *Revelation*, uses to designate the message he communicates. It is a revelation, an unveiling, an uncovering. God is unveiled as the author and finisher of the course of human history (1:8); the initiator and fulfiller of the course of world redemption (21:6); and the beginning and the ending of the course of divine judgment (22:13). God's plan in creation will be consummated, Christ's work of salvation will be concluded, the Holy Spirit will effect the work of restoring God's image. Apocalypse is the unveiling of the meaning of the present in the light of the final end. The only way to understand the real meaning of the present is in the light of the future.

Smith finds similarities between Christian and black American apocalyptic traditions in their willingness to embrace the irony of forgiveness and reconciliation on the one hand and divine wrath and retribution on the other. In the latter aspect, that in the end, the *eschaton* (Greek for "last things"), there is the carryover "from slave religion into the twentieth century in various forms and permutations."[47] These also constitute expressions of African American spirituality.

James Cone, in *Black Theology and Black Power*, illustrates the continuity of the tradition of spirituality of the slave ancestors for African Americans, explaining that Jesus came "into the very depths of human existence for the sole purpose of striking off the chains of slavery, thereby freeing [humankind] from ungodly principalities and powers that hinder [its] relationship with God."[48]

The conventions through which African American spirituality finds expressions are many, but again, a common core of expression seems to be found consistently in the black religious experience: full sensory engaging worship, intimate prayer, cathartic shouting, triumphant singing, politically relevant religious education, and prophetic imaginative preaching. However, as we have pointed out consistently, it is impossible to discuss the religious experience without referencing how profoundly it affects the total life of African Americans. So in the arts—literature, poetry, music, dance, sculpture—there are manifestations of the spirituality of African Americans.

Much has been written about each of the conventions. Full sensory engaging worship, inclusive of music and triumphant singing, has been explored by many observers.[49] The importance of music for African Americans reaches back to the slave period. Toward the end of the eighteenth century, missionaries realized that the only way to succeed in converting the slaves to Christianity was through the use of music. They recognized that the African slaves were unwilling to give up their worldview and musical practices for Christianity. So they began to incorporate the musical practices of the slaves whenever they provided religious instruction, and especially during worship. Prophetic imaginative preaching has been examined extensively in recent decades.[50] W. E. B. DuBois, as early as 1903, stated that "the preacher is the most unique personality developed by the Negro on American soil. A leader, a politician, an orator, a 'boss,' an intriguer, an idealist—all these (they) are and ever, too, the center of a group of men (and women), now twenty, now a thousand in number."[51] Politically relevant religious education can be seen in the works of Martin Luther King Jr. and C. Eric Lincoln and Lawrence Mamiya.[52]

Intimate prayer in African American religion, as in African religion, is all-embracing. No area of human life—or of human experience of joy and praise, pain and happiness—is outside of the realm of prayer. "The physical world is embraced in the arms of the spiritual, the physical is lifted up into the spiritual."[53] In the African American prayer tradition, "God became for them [African Americans] the supreme ruler of heaven and earth, and [God] could do anything but fail. God was the one who acted in the lives of the [parents] and would not default on their prayers and faithfulness . . . nor in the lives of their sons and daughters."[54]

Prayer is more than a ritual or a set of specific prayers. It is the belief that God hears all sincere prayers, prayers that tell God "all about our troubles." Among African Americans, as in Africa, when an individual prays, the whole congregation expresses aloud its assent to the contents of the prayer after each pause. The congregation may respond with things like: "Thank you, God," "Jesus."

Liturgy is extremely important in our day and time. There is a whole attempt at a new kind of liturgical movement. The church universal is seeking to recover an understanding of its worship and liturgy. This can be seen in the Roman Catholic church and churches all over the world. The liturgy is being given back to the people. Old rites are being modified. The text and music that indigenous people use are sources for this revival. This is very evident in African American spirituality. It is not just contemporary, but rather goes back to the traditional religious experience of Africans. We can see it even today in much of what we do in our churches. We need also to resist attempts to reduce expressions of our experiences with God to merely emotional (sometimes understood as "spiritual") activities. We need to affirm that encounter with God and exposure to God is a total human experience.

Franklin suggests that "shouting" as a convention of African American spirituality manifests itself in a whole range of emotional and liberating expressions. There is the notion that some songs cannot be sung if one has not "gone through." Arthur Hall, one of the characters in James Baldwin's *Just above My Head* describes this truth in the African American experience when he says, "Niggers can sing gospel as no other people can because they aren't singing gospel. . . . When a Nigger quotes the Gospel, he's not quoting: he is telling you what happened to him today, and what is going to happen tomorrow. . . . Our suffering is our bridge to one another."[55]

This nexus between life experiences and life tale is ever present. Witnessing, testifying does not allow for fictive generation. This is what Arthur, from *Just above My Head*, is insisting on, "I've got to live the life I sing about in my song."[56] He means that he cannot afford to live a lie. For only by "living the life" is one able to express with any genuineness the pain of life in religion. Some songs elicit a strong emotional response with shouting, jumping up, pointing a finger. When Willa Mae sings, "Nobody knows the trouble I've seen, nobody knows my sorrow . . . ," the congregation knew and identified with what she was singing, so they shouted affirmations and encouragement, "Sing your song, Willa Mae!" "Yes! mmmm! Yes!" In a real sense it was *their* story as well. For to be captured by the dynamism of the religious experience is to compliment the orchestration of that experience which is one's own work in concert with other believers.[57]

As we consider these conventions, we would agree with Franklin that what needs to be explored is "not just shouting as a behavior, but also an experience that provides meaning for participants; a kind of spiritual existential reality shared by all of humanity,"[58] for shouting is an ecstatic experience. The word "ecstasy" comes from a Latin word meaning "to stand outside of"—outside of oneself and out of body. It is truly an experience of possession by the spirit. Spirit possession in African traditional religions has been well documented.

An extremely important aspect of the nurturing process for African American spirituality is seen in the rudiments of black theology and the black church. Grant Shockley examines this in an article on "black theology." He points out that "black theology developed right in the midst of the black struggle for liberation."[59] He affirms that the civil rights struggle and movement nurtured an emerging black theology. Joseph Washington's work on *Black Religion* can also be considered a seminal contribution to this understanding. Shockley sees the historical development of this whole movement as having three distinct phases. First, from 1966 to 1970, the critical voice of the traditional black church was sounded. Second, from 1970 to 1975 additional books, monographs, and articles were developed around black theology, and a Society for the Study of Black Religion was established. Third, in the period beginning in 1975, Cecil Cone's book *The Identity Crisis in Black Theology* was published; the National Committee of Black Churchmen issued its unity statement; and "The Theology in the Americas" project was begun. All of these efforts contributed to the whole black theology movement and consequently to our understanding of African American spirituality.

As we have noted elsewhere, with African American spirituality, there is always the tendency toward wholeness, toward unity. As we look at some of the black theologies and black theologians, James Cone, in *Black Theology and Black Power*, is perhaps the first to deal with the liberation theme. In his subsequent writings, Cone has dealt with the theme of reconciliation. In that first book he raged against those things that were holding black people back. Following Cone, J. Deotis Roberts, in *Liberation and Reconciliation*, advocated a form of reconciliation. Major Jones, in *Black Awareness: A Theology of Hope*, has done the same. Among theologians and scholars in religion, Charles Long has written from a wider religious context and has moved away from the European or Western dualism, as some of the other theologians have done. Gayraud Wilmore has done the same thing. Cone has dealt mostly with the dualism within the European perspective, but Long and others have explored a wider African perspective and thus given us a more holistic cosmology.

In her seminal work on Christology, *White Women's Christ and Black Women's Jesus,* Jacquelyn Grant makes part of her dedication "to the memory of her grandmother, Mrs. Eliza Ward, who in the stillness of a coma, when she heard the name of Jesus, moved."[60] A brief review of her thesis and the importance of Jesus for African Americans, and particularly African American women is appropriate. It would suggest that feminist theology deals almost exclusively with white women's experience. Because of this perspective and its exploration of a single issue, sexism, it is inadequate for addressing the issues of nonwhite women. Those issues, and particularly for black women, have a "tri-dimensional reality . . . which is characterized by the convergence of racism, sexism and classism."[61] Recognizing this reality permits "the development of holistic theological and christological construction which are wholly rather than partially liberating."[62]

Grant's work reaffirms that for black women and for African Americans in general, the experience of Jesus that is valued is of one who meets them in all the varying circumstances of life. Life is not a collection of separate fragments but an integrated whole. We may even dare to claim that when Eliza Ward moved at the name of Jesus, it was a recollection of who Jesus was for her in all those situations of life. As Grant testifies, "The love and kindness, the giving and the sacrifices, and the community service and political interest we witnessed in our parents were in the name of Jesus."[63]

African American Spirituality and Hidden Wholeness

African American spirituality is the persistent desire of a people to tell its story. Essentially it is testimony or public confession and witness. It takes many forms and is expressed in many ways. Yet there is always the connection between individual and community. Although public testimony places the individual "I" at the center of the story, it is really a variant of the group's autobiography. Public testimony, telling the story, however painful, becomes a necessary ritual both for catharsis and freedom. It eventually leads to *kinesis*, energy, and communal celebration.

John in James Baldwin's *Go Tell It on the Mountain* discovers the whole history of his people while on the threshing floor, and the voices of the chanting sisters become in the subliminal ear "a sound of rage and a weeping from time set free." This movement in and down, this descent into the interior is not escape from surface reality into fantasy. Rather, it is a descent beneath the present reality into the rediscovered rhythms connected with the historic experience of the people.

In this chapter we have tried to identify what we consider the essence of an African American spirituality. It differs from a more Eurocentric worldview. It emerged from a people whose pain and suffering has been almost unbearable.

All the studies to which we have referred and what we learned from students who shared their stories in our classrooms confirm some common themes. They all suggest a weaving together of pain, suffering, sense of community, networking, struggle, survival, and hope. Indeed, they are all part of our human existence, of life itself. And life for Africans and African Americans is an undifferentiated whole. To fragment human life and experience is to frustrate the wholeness God intends. Failing to acknowledge the possibility that hidden wholeness exists creates existential emptiness. Life is meant to be lived fully, to be a wholesome experience. To live fully is to begin to recognize one's humanity by looking at oneself but equally by looking at others with the compassion that God gives.

We have shown that the several and varied experiences of African Americans can contribute to an understanding of spirituality, of hidden wholeness. The tale that those experiences tell is, as Baldwin suggests, "the only light in all this darkness." But more than that, in the lineage of the African tradition, African American religious experience, responding to the contextual realities on American soil from slavery through the present, has reflected not only the communal but the integration of life, interweaving work, play, and worship; nature, history, and spirit. As we pursue the task we have set for ourselves, we will draw on the understandings of African American spirituality. It is a spirituality that fosters joy and celebration even in the midst of pain. It may be a spirituality that is needed in a world torn apart with great human suffering. It is that world which we will examine in chapter 3.

Questions for Reflection and Action

1. Some persons think it is mere sentimentality for African Americans to point to Africa and celebrate their cultural heritage. If you disagree, what are some important statements you would offer to support your position?

2. In what ways have the intertwining of music and religion served to sustain African Americans in slave and free societies? Give some examples from your knowledge of history.

3. Read again the words of the spiritual, "Oh, Freedom," (*Songs of Zion*, 102). In what ways do you think those words express the African American ancestors' understanding of who and whose they were and would be? How do those words help African Americans today to express deep convictions and shape the way in which they live life in the world?

4. "Telling the story," "testifying," and "witnessing" express ways in which daily life and the journey of faith come together for African Americans. Reflect on this for yourself, then record or tell a recent and significant experience that illustrates this truth for you.

5. Identify those places and opportunities in the life of the congregation with which you are affiliated where practices in spirituality reflect the African heritage. How do those practices enhance or hinder the faith development of persons?

6. The psalmist testifies out of his loneliness and forsakenness how he was comforted, when he cries out: "you have given me the heritage of those who fear your name" (Ps. 61:5). Among them (the people of God) he was "somebody." How does this scripture offer clues for your self-identity as someone who believes in God and also is African American? Can you list other biblical texts that African American slave ancestors used in self-affirmation?

3

"Dis Howlin' Wildaness"
Our Present Reality

> We is gathahed hyeah, my brothahs,
> In dis howlin' wildaness,
> Fu' to speak some words of comfo't
> To each othah in distress.
> An' we chooses fu' ouah subjic'
> Dis—we'll 'splain it by an' by;
> "An' de Lawd said, 'Moses, Moses,'
> An' de man said, 'Hyeah am I.'"[1]

African Americans were led into the desert experience through slavery. The early black preachers, writers, singers, and dramatists portrayed the "howlin' wildaness" for us over and over again in their works.

The howling desert experience is not only embodied in African American spirituality; it resounds throughout the history of spirituality, where the dark night of the soul is a recurring theme. Because Jesus was led into the desert and suffered, so we, his followers, are also to suffer. Early slaves, in trying to give meaning to their agony, could easily share vicariously with Jesus in the desert. The desert experience was the ultimate in spirituality for slaves.

The transcendent and the immanent became one. The desert thus represents the garden of God. Though the slave suffered, the "wildaness" was filled with trees, springs, lakes, and fruit. The metaphorical wilderness was filled with music, dance, and preaching and was thus transformed into a garden.

Out of the desert experience, the slave also achieved a bonding and relatedness that could only come from pain and suffering. For the black antebellum preacher, the sermon was spirituality because it was preached out of the concrete reality of slavery. It had a method of correlating the biblical text and the contemporary situation. The preacher was adept at using humor to make sermonic points, and sermons always offered consolation: God was in the midst of oppression and of every troubling, painful, hurting life experience, even death. James Weldon Johnson's "Go Down, Death" is a good example. In that poetic drama, the preacher is helping his hearers to realize that death does bring an ending to all the troubles of this world. Sister Caroline recognized that, so that when she saw Old Death, she wasn't frightened, but instead welcomed him like an old friend who was taking her home.[2] To appreciate the force and power of the narrative, black preaching is best heard. With great oratorical skills, the black antebellum preacher so dramatized a story that listeners could identify with the words. In a real sense, such preaching drew persons into community—an essential characteristic of African American spirituality.

The spirituals and the blues, which are but "secular spirituals,"[3] have given many African Americans a way to claim black dignity and humanity in the midst of great oppression and pain. The spirituals and that antebellum sermon "Dis Howlin' Wildaness" remain popular because they point not only to a significant past but also to a present reality. People of African descent are no longer formally enslaved, and many social, political, and economic changes have occurred that have lessened the effects of segregation and the disfranchisement of African Americans. Yet in some important ways, we are not out of the wilderness. Throughout the world and even in the United States, we are confounded with a present social reality that can grieve even the least sensitive persons among us.

Economic Injustice: Have Gots and Have Nots

The majority of the whole human family does not enjoy the standard of living that we demand in the United States. Approximately two-thirds of the world's population, those who have been categorized as "Third World," live in conditions that we would describe as being poor or impoverished. They are women, men, boys, and girls who experience "high infant mortality and low life expectancy due to the lack of food, clothing and shelter."[4] They are poor, says Sister Marie Augusta Neal, because they have an "unequal access to the food, energy and materials needed to provide shelter, security and human development."[5] Their common experience is the human experience of being poor.

There are exceptions to this general statement. There is a small percentage of adults and children in the less developed or "Two-Thirds World," who are among the "non-poor"—those persons "with low infant mortality rates and high life expectancy, those above the poverty line, or more simply, those who are well fed."[6] There are children and adults in the United States and other more economically advantaged countries who have an existence that is basically poor. But for the most part, the majority of people living in the southern hemisphere (with exceptions like Australia), among the developing nations of the world, are poor. This is the rule, not the exception.

In Asia, the Middle East, most of Africa, and in large parts of Central and South America, poverty is a relatively general and lasting experience. The vast majority of the population among these nations exists at a minimal level. Starvation is commonplace. Disease spreads because of nutritional deficiencies. A significant percentage of babies and new mothers die. Health care is woefully inadequate. These conditions result in permanently inadequate means of meeting basic human needs. Sheer survival is at best difficult.

It is difficult for those of us in the United States who are not impoverished to accept the truth that we are greatly advantaged. We participate in a North American society which, for the most part, has an abundance of resources. Most of us, most of the time have the food, energy, and materials required for shelter, security, and human development. It is painful to witness, through our various media sources, the plight among the world's people, especially those whose experience differs significantly from our own. It is more painful still to consider that their economic conditions are a result of worldwide economic injustice.

Our world and the majority of its family members experience economic injustice even today. They are poor and have very little means of producing wealth. Often they are victims of a world economy which so far has produced a small elite (mostly individuals and groups in the Northern hemisphere) that maintains the means of production which in turn produces wealth. A primary source of economic injustice in our world is "the concentration of ownership of production assets and the consequent ability to use those assets to further the narrow aims of the elite"[7] rather than for the well-being of those persons and groups outside this small, elite group of persons.

We have become somewhat more aware of this in the United States in recent years. We read in our newspapers of a chief executive officer earning millions of dollars while in the same company an average worker earns a comparative pittance—even if his or her job has not been eliminated through buyouts and corporate mergers. Job loss or the fear of it has become commonplace in our society.

As is the case on a world scale, this contributes to the formation of two fairly distinctive groups of people: the rich and the poor. The very rich or wealthy are few, but appear to maintain a concentration of power and accumulated wealth. This has become glaring in the United States.

> In our society, roughly 80% of the income arising from production is paid out in wages and salaries, while the other 20% is property income in the form of rent, interest, and profit. This property income is paid to those who own the means of production. For example, in the United States today, fully 60% of that ownership is concentrated among 1% of the population. In fact, 90% of the population owns no such assets at all. Therefore, one-fifth of all income goes to a very small segment of the population.[8]

This small, elite class of people effectively controls our surplus production. They have accumulated wealth which enables them to accumulate even more. They control our present-day means of production and will be the only ones able to create future ones. Hence, over time, they will increase their wealth and resultant economic power. Economic injustice is a stark reality in the United States and in our world. This is also the case when we consider the impact of racism.

Racism: Masters and Slaves Continuing?

In many ways, racism, as an institutional form, is a fairly modern phenomenon. The ideology of white supremacy really did not take hold until Europeans came into close contact with other races, particularly the African race. When men and women, mostly from the Northern Hemisphere, encountered peoples of the Southern Hemisphere, modern racism, as we know it, took hold. The doctrine of white supremacy and black inferiority, in terms of authority and legitimacy, is at the very core of modern forms of racism. This fundamentally erroneous belief has perpetuated untold suffering, death, and near extinction of many peoples of color. The majority of the human race are people of color. A minority consisting mostly of light-skinned Europeans have attempted from the early sixteenth century, through various manifestations of institutionalized racism, to reinforce this white supremacist ideology.

This has been the same story for many centuries. Europeans and European Americans invaded the habitat of "Two-Thirds World" people for centuries. The Atlantic slave trade and the institution of slavery forcibly took from Africa "between 3.5 million to over 50 million Africans," and "for every African who survived the rigors of transport to the New World about five others died."[9] Colonization produced the taking of land, resources and people. In fact, prior to 1945, the overwhelming majority of "Two-Thirds World" people were under Western domination. That changed radically between 1945 and 1970, but it illustrates significant historical oppression. The genocide of American Indians occurred during similar periods. The ongoing attempt by some to oppress and dominate others has been a reality of our existence. The assumption of white supremacy has remained endemic in our modern world. Cornel West, a genealogist of modern racism, affirms that this is the case:

> The notion that black people are human beings is a relatively new discovery in the modern West. The ideal of black equality in beauty, culture, and intellectual capacity remains problematic and controversial within prestigious halls of learning and sophisticated intellectual circles. The Afro-American encounter with the modern world has been shaped first and foremost by the doctrine of white supremacy, which is embodied in institu-

tional practices and enacted in everyday folkways under varying circumstances and evolving conditions.[10]

The modern racist worldview is based on the perspective that a
person's or a group of persons' inherent worth is judged on the basis of the individual or collective genes. One's genetic structure defines who one is, according to this ideology. Men and women who
are racist feel superior to or of greater worth than others who have
a different genetic structure—facial features, hair color, or skin
color. The racist assumption is maintained in such a way that the
sense of one's own worth and the worth of others can be grounded
in genes. Ethnocentrism, or prejudice based on differences in culture, has been with us for a long time. But the doctrine of white supremacy is fairly recent—perhaps during the last five hundred years.
Certainly the so-called scientific ranking or classification of the vari-
ations in our human family has occurred only since the late seven-
teenth century. The arrogant and divisive cancer that is eating at the
core of our human world community—that belief that some groups
or categories of human beings are biologically or genetically inferior
to others—is a relatively modern phenomenon. Joseph Barndt ar-
ticulates our dilemma, when he says:

> Racism is perhaps the major moral issue of the twenty-first
> century. It weaves a negative web of bigotry, hate, and violence;
> it makes us all victims in a worldview that is marked by greed,
> wealth, exploitation, and oppression. It makes us all captives
> in an imprisoning vision that cannot work and servants to an
> old world order that must be dismantled.[11]

Racism takes various forms in our society and world. It is different from or more than racial prejudice, hatred, or discrimination. It
often takes on institutional form. We continue to see this in resi-
dential segregation by housing and the real estate industry. The
banks of our country reinforce this with the illegal, but seemingly
common practice of "redlining." Persons of color, and housing areas where persons of color presently live, are blocked from the usual
lines and opportunity of credit. Two of our seminary colleagues experienced this discriminatory practice recently in their effort to build

a new home. Both had Ph.D.s, excellent credit, and a sizable down payment. Until they worked with an African American-owned bank, they were systematically blocked, for several months, from moving ahead. Institutional racism remains even when laws exist to supposedly eliminate its reality. "Eighty-six percent of white suburban Americans live in neighborhoods that are less than one percent black."[12]

Other forms of institutional racism persist. Hate groups like the Ku Klux Klan, the Aryan Nation, and the skinheads are thriving in our modern world. The burning of over forty black churches in the South in the last five years is a most recent and recurring expression of racism in our society. Schools in the United States are still, in significant ways, segregated. Discriminatory employment and promotion policies underscore racist behavior. Textbooks are still developed and used in our educational institutions which ignore or distort the role of most people of color. The majority of newspapers and radio and television stations are controlled by European Americans. And *control* is the key issue.

While there may be forms of black prejudice and discrimination in our daily lives, white racism is a one-of-a-kind reality. Racism manifests itself when power and prejudice are linked. This in no way suggests that black men and women do not have power. They do in so many ways: economically, socially, politically, culturally, and individually. And yet the major institutions of our society—government, business, industry, unions, churches, and educational settings—are, for the most part, dominated by white individuals and groups. When one combines institutional power with racial discrimination, the result is institutional racism.

How can one explain the conditions of American society without taking into account institutionalized racism? How does one attempt to explain that African Americans' income in the United States is approximately 60 percent of whites'? In other words, for every dollar a white worker receives for job-related compensation, an African American worker will receive approximately sixty cents.[13] How are we to understand the fact that the poverty rate among blacks is three to one in America? What explanation can we offer for a 40 percent teenage unemployment rate within the black community? How do we justify the assertion that a black university graduate will make less money during his or her lifetime than an average white high school graduate?[14] How do we live with the awareness of an imprisonment rate for African Americans that is six times that of whites?[15] What do we do with homicide statistics indicating that in "1990, a young white male's statistical likelihood of becoming a victim of homicide is roughly 1 chance in 186, while a young black male's statistical chances are 1 in 20?"[16] If these indicators or statistics are not evidence of institutionalized racism, then we have become blind to the truth. The truth is that we live in a racist society and world. It is a world that assumes a doctrine of white supremacy.

A small and very readable book recently came off the press with a very interesting title: *Never Say Nigger Again! An Antiracism Guide for White Liberals*.[17] It is the contribution of one woman, M. Garlinda Burton, to help those who are serious and intentional about addressing racism in our society and in the denomination to which she belongs. Burton is the editor of *Interpreter: Program Ideas for United Methodists*. Before assuming that position, she had served for over a decade as director of the Nashville office of the United Methodist News Service, where she specialized in racial and gender issues. Out of her experience in these areas the book arises. The book has very useful and practical suggestions. In extremely plain and direct language, Burton invites readers to confront and embrace their emotional realities. She challenges "well-meaning white people who do not deal with their *unique* brand of unintentional and unconscious racism"[18] to remove those obstacles. And in a final appeal, she asks her readers to "believe in the power of good over the ills of racism, and believe that your one altered life can make a big difference."[19]

To make a commitment to such a vision and to be engaged in liberating action, we firmly believe, will help persons so engaged begin to discover the hidden wholeness.

"Ain't I a Woman?": Women's Struggle for Affirmation and Respect

Racism and sexism represent institutional evils which appear to be built into the very structure of the United States. Certain physical characteristics, which are a given at one's birth, suggest a kind of permanency to the classification of individuals. Here again, gene structure comes into play. Sexism, like racism, attempts to categorize human beings based on biological or genetic bases—in this case gender. Sexual bias seems to precede racial bias, historically. In fact, "the oppression of women, as the oldest form of subjugation in human history," may serve "as a model for other kinds of oppression."[20]

Sexism is less modern than is racism. It appears to be deeply rooted in our Western philosophical and religious traditions. "Sexual differences have been viewed as creations of God, and sexual inequality has frequently been viewed as God-ordained. Hence, the meaning system has often reinforced gender roles (tasks designated as 'women's work' or 'men's work') and concepts of gender (concepts of 'masculinity' or 'femininity')."[21]

Early in our history women and children were placed under the domination of men. The paternalistic order of preindustrial societies supported this hierarchical order of the human creature. The criterion for measuring the value and status of persons has been and is at present the dominant political group in our society—white, usually economically privileged, males.

"Women, like (black) slaves, were deprived of the right to vote, legal rights over their property and custody of their children, educational opportunities, and were virtually excluded from participation in government, business, and the professions.[22] Even after emancipation, the subordination of women, similar to that of African Americans, has been powerful. Characteristic sexist assumptions about brain size; intellectual ability; "place" in the home, work world, and society have been maintained by many, especially those holding power positions in our society. When a culture, like our Western one, defines men as the bearers of authority, power, and value to the exclusion of women—a basic androcentric position—that culture is in trouble. It is a condition that suggests we are truly not out of the wilderness yet!

Women in the late twentieth century have experienced varying degrees of liberation, especially so in the more developed settings of our world. However, politically, socially, and economically, the world that women experience is not the same as the one men encounter. Statistically, the world of women has been one of imbalance. There are great inequities between the genders in the United States and in our world.

There are many ways to illustrate the condition of women in the world at large. It has been said that "women constitute half the world's population, perform nearly two-thirds of its work hours, receive one-tenth of the world's income, and own less than one-hundredth of the world's property."[23] In other words, basic economic discrepancies between men and women of the world illustrate sexist realities.

The legal status of women is also problematic. For the most part, women do not have the same legal or constitutional rights as men. True, "the legal provision of rights does not guarantee 'equality,' but it is an essential prerequisite for women's full participation in political, economic, social and cultural development, from which equality can follow."[24]

Poverty is another indicator of sexist social realities. Throughout the world, the largest poverty group is the one characterized by woman-headed households. Poverty has been and continues to be feminized. In the United States, 78 percent of all people living in poverty are women or children under the age of eighteen; in Australia, the proportion is 75 percent; in Canada, 60 percent of all women over age sixty-four live in poverty.[25]

There are numerous other ways to point to the social conditions of women and their oppressive reality. Domestic violence is perpetuated to "keep women in their place." Female genital mutilation is still practiced with regularity in major parts of our world, especially in Africa and the Middle East. Women teach in primary school teachers, but significantly fewer teach in universities. Women in both Haiti and Japan constitute less than 6 percent of all employees in the news media. "In Peru and Canada, in the UK and Uruguay, women have the same proportion of representation in government."[26] In so-called developed countries and those reported to be "developing," women experience great inequalities. There are really no "developed" countries for women!

The sexist reality of our society and world community produces a condition that points to a similar pattern among women. Everywhere it appears, women are worse off than men.

Women have less power, less autonomy, more work, less money, and more responsibility. Women everywhere have a smaller share of the pie; if the pie is very small (as in poor countries), women's share is smaller still. Women in rich countries have a higher standard of living than do women in poor countries, but nowhere are women equal to men.[27]

While women represent the vast majority of congregational members, they continue to be denied significant leadership roles in the church—including pastoral leadership. It is past time that the church of Jesus Christ take a lead in modeling a spirituality that is liberating—one that leads to an affirmation of hidden wholeness.

Trapped by Fear, Targeted for Grace: Helen's Tale

In her junior year at college, Helen got married to get away from home. She eloped. Her growing up was filled with much pain. She had been born to parents who married because of pregnancy. Under these circumstances, she became a "target child"—one destined to be the source of constant dispute in the home. It was from this situation that she ran into marriage.

But marriage sometimes does not offer easy solutions. Helen's marriage produced two sons but no solutions. Rather, Helen experienced and endured eleven years of battery and abuse. When she reflected long and hard on her situation and resolved to change it, internal questions arose: "Why do I want to leave? What about the children? Am I not thinking about the children?" And the external questions from society and church came to mind. At the police station, where she had gone to take out a warrant against her husband, she was met with indifference, unconcern, moralizing: "Why do you want to leave?" And in the church (with no personal relationship to Jesus Christ in her life): "You made your bed, you lie in it." The value, the standard, the pressure: "To be whole, to be healthy, is to be married."

But marriage sometimes does *not* offer easy solutions. Yet Helen

tried again. And with marriage came a procession of problems—
spousal abuse, demonstrated in issues of power and control; failure
in a joint business venture; loss of home; bankruptcy; a son caught
in the entanglements of drugs.

It is strange (or is it?) how in deep crisis a soul makes explorations
into God. Or could it be that we experience the encounter, hear the
voices, feel free to raise the questions because God gives us of the
Divine Self? So in moments of deepening self-awareness, from her
soul's depths, Helen heard: "If you don't do something, you will be
in a catatonic state in a rocking chair, just rocking."

From that encounter with and revelation from God, Helen went
into a three-day period of fasting and prayer. It was then also that
she began journaling—a practice that she has maintained over the
years. It helps not only to record her thoughts, but also her feelings,
her wrestlings, her questions, her answers. From that season of fasting, she received affirmations from God: that God loved her, that
God cared about her life situations, that God was present with and
for her in those situations. This was followed by a command: "You
need to get up and move."

The soul's journey with God begins as response to that command.
It continues through a series of encounters and calls from God to reflect and obey and act. And each soul determines the obedience it
must give, the choices it must make, the openness it must have to
discern and follow God's leading. For as Helen learned then and
continues to discover, "the journey to health and wholeness" demands a singleness of purpose, determining, as Helen states, "I'm
not going to let anything hinder me."

Helen began daily walks by the river, "me and God." Out of those
ventures she discovered the difference between being alone and being lonely. In those encounters with God, Helen was shown how
"every time I had a crisis, my mother was there." She also learned
to recognize and acknowledge emerging support from those others
on the journey of discovery of hidden wholeness. It is a journey to
self-discovery, that God does not make any clones. We are the stories we tell, of the choices that we make, in surrender to God. God
invites us to find God not only in all of life's circumstances and situations, but also in community and with others.

Class, Race, and Gender: Triune Challenge

Economic injustice, racism, and sexism manifest themselves in quite visible ways in our rural and urban communities across the United States. In a society that boasts of significant and open opportunities for all, the increase of homelessness and poverty in this country contradicts those supposed claims. In any of our cities, one can see homeless women, men, and children on a regular basis. People are hungry and exist in the most dire circumstances. There are churches, synagogues, and mosques that attempt to respond to the basic needs of our homeless population, but the numbers of people are simply too great. Programs that provide food and shelter are important but do not address the more fundamental problems of economic injustice, racism, and sexism.

An alarming number of men and women, girls and boys in our United States simply live on the edge. The "feminization of poverty" in North America and the overwhelming number of children who live in the throes of poverty are devastating realities that cannot be ignored. Our country uses approximately 40 percent of the world's resources while representing only 7 percent of the world's population. Many among our U.S. population do not see or experience this disproportionate share of the world's goods. Like many among the "Two-Thirds World" peoples, they fall victims to the greed and oppressive power of a small minority of persons. They, like their brothers and sisters in other countries, are overwhelmingly people of color, especially women and children. There are many men living on the streets in the United States, but they are mostly African Americans.

Significant numbers of European Americans live on the street or in conditions of poverty, but the disproportionately high percentage of poor or homeless persons who are people of color is incredible. To understand this in any other way than to admit that our system has often failed us—especially those among us who are black, both women and men, boys and girls—is to lie to ourselves. Too many racist, sexist, and economically elitist arguments have been used to blame the victims for their own victimization. This hegemonic and oppressive falsehood will no longer work. Homelessness, hunger, poverty, and the like are simply manifestations of the deeper societal problems we have identified. Even the violence and crime that we witness in our society and the related problem of rampant substance abuse are evidences of deeper problems.

To do violence is to deny fundamentally to another person that which she or he is rightly due as a human being. We generally think of violence as causing bodily harm. But even before that harm occurs, there is the violence of thinking that another is unworthy of the sacredness of personhood, unworthy to be a human being made in the image of God. This kind of thinking and its expression in words and deeds may have festered over time. It subsequently becomes explosive in destructive action.

In Violation: Moriah's Tale

Moriah is an African American woman who has identified her suffering as a vehicle through which she has experienced "a peace that passeth all understanding" and a joy that has led to a newfound spirituality.[28] She has experienced profound suffering through the heartache of suicide and attempted murder. We hope that her story will help to articulate a profound understanding of how suffering and joy relate to African American spirituality. Her experience supports a perspective that suffering, joy, and spirituality are uniquely tied together in the African American community.

Moriah is a well-respected person in the Atlanta, Georgia, community. Approximately two years ago she found herself in a bitter conflict with her husband. As a result of that situation, her life was threatened on several occasions. This situation climaxed when her husband tried to murder her and subsequently committed suicide.

At the age of seventeen, she was impregnated by her boyfriend, David, who later became her husband. At this point in her life she says that her relationship with her grandparents began to suffer. Still, she proudly admits that their relationship was soon repaired. She attributes this reconciliation to the fact that the community concept of her family was greater than the actions of any individual. According to Moriah, the community was foremost in her family.

Moriah married David at the age of twenty-two. She says that David was shy and insecure when she married him. Still, according to Moriah, their marriage began with great promise. She smiles as she recalls the first years of their marriage. However, she explains that for whatever reasons her husband's insecurities began to increase. Ironically, she believes that her newfound commitment to her church contributed to his insecurities. According to Moriah, she began spending most of her leisure time working with different ministries in her church.

It was her opinion that these activities provided her the spiritual growth that she had longed for since leaving her grandparents' home. She added that her husband became extremely jealous of the time she spent working with the church. And to her dismay, he refused to involve himself in similar activities. He also began separating himself from the family and began to physically and mentally abuse her. This abuse occurred repeatedly for several years. She recalls the pain being almost too great to bear. To cope with this problem, she spent as much time as possible reading the Bible and praying that God would deliver her. She says that this process created a joy in her life that seemed possible only through suffering.

On January 5, 1990, the problem culminated in a horrible tragedy. Moriah recalls the incident vividly and quite compassionately. After seeing her husband earlier that day, she remembered feeling a calm that she believed was the Holy Spirit. Later that evening, while driving to the grocery store, she noticed a car following her. She felt intuitively that it was David driving the car. Assuming that David wanted to talk things over, she drove to the next parking lot and parked her car. She remembers that before she could open her car door, David stood in front of it. He then shot her several times in the head. She knew instantly that her faith in God would be severely tested.

Although Moriah has experienced a tremendous sense of personal spiritual growth, she admits that her community played a vital role in that growth. Comparatively, the African American community is holistic in scope. Therefore, it identifies itself with those in the community who suffer.

Moriah says that without the support of others her spiritual understanding might not have been so optimistic. She tells how her immediate family, relatives, church members, coworkers, and other persons in the community supported her during this experience. They gave her money, time, and talent. She remembers the numerous prayers that were prayed over her, and the numerous Bible verses that were read to her. She recalls a coworker's encouragement and a friend spending countless numbers of hours with her while she was in the hospital. She admits that this communal experience was special. However, she candidly acknowledges that she has witnessed similar actions by the community on several other occasions. Moriah also says that through the support of the community she understood that suffering by the faithful would result in growth. As a result of her growth, she presently ministers to battered women. She says that through this ministry she continues to increase in faith and wisdom in God.

Suffering, joy, and spirituality are inextricably tied together in the African American community. Although this perspective is not limited to the African American community, it is a vital theology that can add to the spiritual fervor of other religious expressions throughout the world. The African American understanding of suffering, joy, and spirituality has been the foundation on which the community has based its survival, mainly because they (joy, suffering, and spirituality) are common experiences that the community has accepted holistically.

Too Much Hopelessness, Too Little Hope

Too many of our people are unemployed or underemployed. Far too many of our young men and women experience life in terms of its horrifying meaninglessness, lovelessness, and hopelessness. This nihilistic condition is at the heart of the black experience in the United States. It is a reality, says Cornel West, that threatens our very existence.

> The frightening result is a numbing detachment from others and a self-destructive disposition toward the world. Life without meaning, hope, and love breeds a cold-hearted, mean-spirited outlook that destroys both the individual and others. . . . The major enemy of black survival in America has been and is neither oppression nor exploitation but rather the nihilistic threat—that is, loss of hope and absence of meaning. For as long as hope remains and meaning is preserved, the possibility of overcoming oppression stays alive. The self-fulfilling prophecy of the nihilistic threat is that without hope

there can be no future, that without meaning there can be no struggle.[29]

People representing all ethnic communities have for years used alcohol and other drugs to anesthetize their awareness of the reality of their condition—both external social realities (racism, sexism, and economic deprivation) and internal personal demons (meaningless, hopelessness, and lovelessness). The extremely high levels of alcoholism witnessed among American Indians today is but another representation of these more profound social conditions. Native peoples were cheated, killed, and then manipulated into apartheid levels of existence years ago. They, like others, have too often been thrust into a nihilism seen across our land.

Our politicians appropriate money for the building of prisons, and meagerly increase funding for police protection but systematically avoid the deeper realities of our social and personal existence. There is a relationship between our societal problems and their deeper causes. There is an even more fundamental need that certainly must be addressed.

A World Disenchanted

Max Weber, the esteemed German sociologist, liked to quote Friedrich Schiller's phrase, the "disenchantment" of the world, to describe the significant societal changes that have occurred in modern life. He included this phrase in his discussion of religion and society to characterize a process by which things once held in reverence or awe are, over time, stripped of their special qualities. What was once sacred and revered is deemed "ordinary." Thus, meaning and feelings of belonging are reduced and lessened for the individual and members of society. Roman Catholicism, with its world of angels, shrines, saints, holy days, and holy objects, becomes less powerful in the lives of people with the advent of Protestantism. Hence, Protestantism brought about degrees of disenchantment for what Catholicism has held in reverence.

Rational science promotes disenchantment when it explains certain natural phenomena that previously were attributed to miracles. Beliefs and belief systems maintained by religious bodies become less authoritative, in that questions previously answered by religion are now more often dealt with by science. The world of meaning, beliefs, and a sense of belonging are affected by what Weber calls the "disenchantment" of the world. That which was held as more sacred becomes more secular.

Our analysis of the present world is similar, in that we argue that spirituality in our time is taken less seriously and leaves individuals and communities feeling frustrated. What may have been felt or thought concerning a spiritual dimension of existence is less pervasive and not held in common by the masses. Mystery, awe, that which was or is considered sacred or spiritual, slowly loses its credence.

We contend that there are several factors that have contributed to this state of disenchantment. Several processes have come with modernity to undermine our spiritual awareness. Many books and articles have been written about these complex processes; however, we will simply attempt to highlight their key elements. The impact of the European Enlightenment will be considered. The influences of individualism, privatization, and pluralism will be briefly explored. Dualism, already considered in the first chapter, will be suggested within this context. These and other factors, we argue, must be taken into account when examining the present "disenchanted" state of our world. They must be taken seriously because they point to a fundamental crisis within our world—the absence of a hidden wholeness. This missing hidden wholeness influences our present social reality, and we must discover or rediscover it if we are to confront adequately our racist, sexist, and economically unjust society.

The modern period began with what has been called the Enlightenment, the second great challenge to Western religion (the Reformation was the first). Whereas the Reformation challenged the unity, holiness, and apostolicity of the Roman Catholic church, the Enlightenment challenged the supernatural character of the Protestant church. It pushed the Protestant critique of central religious authority to an extreme.

In earlier periods, the church and its religious claims held ab-

solute authority which was rarely questioned. The traditional Christian acceptance of authority, though, was questioned with the use of
scientific skepticism, especially a skepticism regarding religion.

Copernicus, Galileo, Descartes, Newton, and Locke are persons
we associate with this period. They laid the foundation for a radically new way of viewing the world—one significantly different
from either Catholics or Protestants of that day. It was a more secular view of the world, one that placed control and ultimate destiny
in the hands of the human creature and gave less concern for the
truth claims of revealed religion. It obviously posed a great threat to
religious authority. These early thinkers pushed religion out of the
middle of its earlier central authoritative position.

During the period some call the Age of Reason, following the beginning of the scientific revolutionary period, a new wave of thought
swept across Europe and eventually America. This period of the Enlightenment is associated with persons like Montesquieu, Voltaire,
Reimarus, Lessing, Kant, Smith, Wollstonecraft, Franklin, and Jefferson. To highlight one example, one must only examine the
thought of Immanuel Kant and his attack on the metaphysical assumption that undergirded classical doctrines of revelation. Kant
did not deny a belief in God but argued that reason could not affirm
the actuality of the revelation of God.

> The consequences of Kant's philosophical program for clas-
> sical theology and for the natural religion of the Enlightenment
> were nothing less than revolutionary. If the existence of God
> could not be demonstrated, and if statements about God (de-
> rived either from reason or from supernatural revelation) bore
> no relation to any empirical object, then the rug had been
> pulled out from under theology. The metaphysical structure on
> which classic models of revelation had been erected was
> thereby destroyed, and an apparently unbudgeable chasm was
> created between theology and the world accessible to reason.[30]

Hence, the Enlightenment thinkers assumed that the rational
mind of the human creature would eventually solve all social problems of human existence. Their goal was to use enlightened thought
to bring about radical societal solutions. They would create a bet-

ter society and world. Science would heal and solve the world's problems. Human creatures would control their environment without the oppressive dictates of one central religious authority. They would make life better for all the inhabitants of the good earth.

Individualism

Individualism would add to the goal; it would preserve the integrity and worth of the individual person. Individualism promised to free the individual self from the constraints of society, family, and marital partnership. It offered the man or woman the opportunity to be autonomous, expressive, assertive, and free. It gives individuals the self-determined authority to decide truth for themselves. It allowed individuals to decide for themselves the religious truth that fit their own lifestyles.

Alexis de Tocqueville, in his *Democracy in America*,[31] raised a warning against the consuming power of individualism which he observed on the American scene. This French social scientist feared that any level of commitment to other citizens or the wider community would eventually be lost to this all-pervasive priority of American individualism.

Jefferson, Franklin, Whitman, and Emerson are significant figures in our American historical landscape who furthered the ideas and concepts of individuals. They, along with others, advanced an individuality that has become an excessive individualism. Robert Bellah and associates[32] have explored the far-reaching implication of individualism. They describe the significant difference this makes on individuals and our society. The way children are raised and encouraged to become separate, autonomous human beings sets great limits on the comprehensiveness of the family. The movement away from a sense of call or communal purpose for work is replaced by career and upward economic- and social-status mobility. Marriage is contractual. Community becomes more individualized based on a lifestyle enclave. Public life is sought only for the purpose of providing self-interest and self-advancement.

The point of this discussion is to illustrate the pervasive nature of individualistic thought and its great impact on American society. The individual becomes a separate autonomous self, moving quickly away from family ties and community bonds. Individuals work for themselves and marry to fulfill contractual needs. Individuals use public life for self-fulfillment.

Religion does not enable the autonomous self to connect to others but enhances the seeking of individual goals and objectives. The church provides an arena where the person is valued as an individual or as one who maintains a personal relationship with God. Community or collective bonds are downplayed. Individual, spiritual, physical, and psychological needs are applauded in their self-fulfillment.

Spirituality that is discovered in community and grounded in a communal and liberating experience is ignored in this individualistic self- and societal understanding. The congregation exists for the personal, not the social, needs of the masses or community. Religious people are self-actualized people not bound by common ties. Corporate worship is simply not that. It is private worship within a group. Spirituality is individually understood and experienced. Spirituality is a private affair. This spirituality or a larger community-based "hidden wholeness" is almost absent. Individualism chokes the life out of community and collective spiritual awareness.

Salvation is thoroughly individualized. The individual soul is important, not the collective spiritual being of society, community, neighborhood or congregation. People attend church and participate in religion to have their private personal needs met. The preaching becomes something based more on psychological content than anything else. The spirit of the isolated, autonomous and self-absorbed individual is the targeted audience, not a spirituality of wholeness that embraces the large community and society. Individualism, like Tocqueville feared, strips the individual and the greater society of its connectedness and leaves both to their eventual demise.

Martin Luther King, Jr. reflects on this theme, with prophetic insight, in his famous "American Dream" speech, as he argues:

> But the shape of the world today does not permit us the luxury of an anemic democracy. The price that America must pay for the continued exploitation of the Negro and other minority groups is the price of its own destruction. The hour is late; the clock of destiny is ticking out. It is trite, but urgently true,

that if America is to remain a first class nation she can no have second class citizens. Now, more than ever before, America is challenged to bring her noble dream to reality, and those who are working to implement the American dream are the true saviors of democracy.[33]

Decades later, we still exhibit a studied reluctance to come to terms with the mutual recognition of a hidden wholeness in our life together in this nation.

Dualism

Along with individualism, dualism is a powerful force in much of North American culture and thought. This system of thought has been present since the time of the Greeks. The Greeks held that the soul was good and the body evil. They saw time as corrupt where eternity was pure. They sought heaven and rejected the earth. They argued for the blessedness of the spirit but rejected the flesh as being impure.

Plato's dualism offered two independent domains: the sensible and the intelligible. The early "desert fathers" and other monastics "retreated from the world and its blandishments, feeling that only in isolated places could God be truly found"[34] and thus adapted Christianity to a Greek worldview. Descartes presented a dualism of thinking and extended substances, while Kant offered a dualism of the noumenal and the phenomenal.[35] Even though the Protestant Reformation sought to protest a two-tiered view of reality, the traditional Lutheran doctrine of "the two realms" at points reinforced it. Protestant hymnody often displays a dualistic worldview when it divides the body and soul, earth and heaven.

The dualism of North American Christianity has been in place for many centuries. Greek thought, early Christianity, and more recent Reformation thinking have all contributed to this understanding. The consequences of this way of viewing the world are great. The separation of the mind and body is especially destructive.

Joseph Hough and John Cobb contend that social and existential consequences are still being felt:

> Sociologically, the mind-body dualism functioned in the bourgeois imagination to exalt the bourgeois individual as mind

and to view those who were unable to realize their individuality as matter. Of course, the official rhetoric attributed mind to all human beings, and this softened the tendency of which we speak. But psychologically and sociologically, it is clear that the individualistic respect for individuals did not extend to the classes and races exploited by capitalism. Instead of effectively realizing the humanistic ideals of the Enlightenment, dualism consciously or unconsciously justified colonialism and even slavery.[36]

They and others argue that the division of the mind and the body, the earth and heaven, the body and the soul, human beings and other life forms, etc., creates a separation of nature and creation that is not only artificial but destructive. The dualism creates a superior domain and an inferior one. It separates the human creature within her/himself. It alienates human beings, where one group or race is seen as dominant. It perpetuates the dominance of nature and the environment by the human animal, who supposedly has a higher position in the created order. Nature is destroyed and abused instead of seen as an integral part of the whole universe.

Africans, as well as other people of color, are seen as lesser beings. Women are considered inferior. American Indians were mistakenly viewed as aggressors and were controlled through forced marches, incarceration on reservations, or annihilation. Dualism sets in motion a separation of human and social existence and thereby contributes to the destruction of the human and ecological connectedness of existence. Any spirituality that permeates the whole of the person, all groups of persons, or the expanded earth is simply not possible. Again, a solitary spirituality that manifests itself in the individual or homogeneous subgroup of creation is all that is possible.

Matthew Fox argues that this dualistic tendency in dominant North American culture

plays kindly into the hands of empire-builders, slave masters, and patriarchal society in general. It divides and thereby conquers, pitting one's thoughts against one's feelings, one's body against one's spirit, one's political vocation against one's personal needs, people against earth, animals and nature in general. By doing this, it so convolutes people, so confuses and preoccupies them, that deeper questions about community, justice, and celebration never come to the fore.[37]

It keeps people from discovering a deeper and more embracing spirituality that unites rather than separates. It undercuts mutuality and interdependence. It stifles creativity within and openness to different groups of people and diverse ways of thinking. It separates the human family and the larger created order. Spirituality that is all-embracing, that unites the created order, one that has depth and breadth and produces a wholeness described in this book is difficult (if not impossible) with this overarching dualism.

Two additional factors that contribute to the disenchantment of the world are pluralism and privatization. Pluralism refers to conditions in the larger society, while privatization deals more with individuals and their private lives.

Pluralism

Pluralism refers to "a societal situation in which no single world view holds a monopoly."[38] In earlier periods of our history certain religions, like Catholicism, held a monopoly over other worldviews. Alternative perspectives or meaning systems were absorbed into the monolithic system. Early monasticism is an example.

Yet today, highly pluralistic societies such as the United States, Canada, and others have several diverse groups with competing worldviews. Several and varied worldviews coexist and compete as plausible alternatives to one another. The result is that all the religious systems lose credibility. "The pluralistic situation relativizes the competing world views and deprives them of their taken-for-granted status." Thus, "in a pluralistic situation," in contrast to earlier periods, "no single world view is inevitable."[39]

In the United States, a committed Roman Catholic's neighbors are Baptist, Jewish, Unitarian, Lutheran, atheist and Zen Buddhist. The government and the society do not (formally, at least) give favorite legitimacy to any of these world views, nor does anyone's god accommodate anybody's quandary by sending down a lightning bolt to get rid of all the "wrong" believers. If people wish to protect the belief that their world view is uniquely true, they must isolate themselves from alternative world views. In American society, especially in relatively urban settings, that is not easy to do. On the job, in school, through the media, working for a political party or a social "cause," or even playing softball—and increasingly in neighborhoods, social clubs, and parties—Americans are exposed to others who hold different world views from their own. The impact of the pluralistic situation is thus that the various world views in society also compete for legitimacy. No single view has such uncontested legitimacy that a person expressing it authoritatively could be certain of being taken seriously.[40]

Thus, pluralization makes society even more complex. It contributes to the reality that no single worldview or cultural consensus is possible. It nurtures the phenomenon we call "privatization" as the individual finding no single truth or cultural consensus looks within the private sphere for meaning.

Privatization

Privatization, like individualism, dualism, and pluralism, contributes to the disenchantment of the world. It produces a religiosity that is privately understood and experienced, leaving little room for a more collective and communal sense of association. The private person, with her or his individually chosen set of beliefs, functions as the sole criterion for what is true and applicable.

Privatization "is the process by which certain differentiated institutional spheres (e.g., religion, family, leisure, the arts) are segregated from the dominant institutions of the public sphere (e.g., economic, political, legal) and relegated to the private sphere."[41] Hence, individuals attempt to find a sense of or sources of identity not in the community, church or society but only in the private sphere. They look less to the public sphere and more to the private. "The individual's very self is privatized."[42]

The consequences of pluralism and privatization are significant. The collapse of any shared worldview results with pluralization. Building consensus and creating public policy is next to impossible. Seeing or feeling one's ties to others is equally difficult in the privatized society. Many isolated and privatized persons coexist in a society of other privatized persons. Building (and experiencing) an interdependent community is seemingly unattainable.

Spirituality that transcends the individual and the particularism of a specific worldview becomes greatly frustrated. Spirituality that is liberating and unifies through a comprehensive wholeness is thwarted. The world becomes more disenchanted.

Thus, the enlightened creature has not fulfilled what he or she had aspired to fulfill. The society that was to evolve has not. The reason that we hoped would free us from many of our problems has not produced great and long-lasting results. The individual can attribute other persons' problems to the lack of individual initiative. Systemic and root causes of poverty, racism, and substance abuse can be ignored with the individualistic eye of the beholder. A dualistic world allows for those who have "superior" insight and personal discipline and those who do not. People can be categorized as those who are responsible and those who are not. Truth can be claimed by anyone, according to any one particular interpretation. Consensus about societal problems and worldwide needs can be seen as only one among many worldviews of reality. The private individual can thank God for blessings privately received and ignore the needs of the masses.

Our thinking and behavior, the elements of our modern worldview—Enlightenment thought, individualistic perspective, dualistic perception, pluralistic and privatized self-understandings—can aid in our avoidance of the world and its problems. They can contribute to our disenchanted world and isolated and impoverished existence. For our individualized and privatized poverty of spirit is similar to the economic and political poverty of so many. Both us and them are indeed impoverished.

Our contemporary social existence may present itself in the forms of economic injustice, racism, and sexism. We contend that below the surface of those devastating realities lies a more crucial and core reality. We are a so-called modern people who live in a world that has become disenchanted. And if we are to challenge the social problem of our existence, and their correlational concerns that appear in our nihilistic environment, we must discover or rediscover a hidden wholeness. As the diagram suggests, that hidden wholeness, we believe, exists; it is present, just not readily recognized. Our private

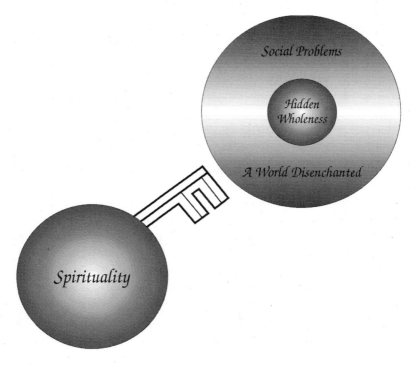

and collective blindness or sin often blocks us from seeing what lies in front of us, behind, below, or above us.

God created us to be whole people and whole communities. It was not God's intention that we choose to relate to one another differently based on race, sex, or class. God did not create us to experience life in a state of meaningless, hopelessness, and lovelessness. In fact, the ground of our hope, the source of our love, and the wellspring of our meaning begins and ends in our Creator. Our Creator God is the author of our misplaced hidden wholeness, that reality we long for and need to live authentic and liberated lives in today's world.

A Hidden Wholeness in Our Midst

The unique spirituality of African Americans offers us a resource that is needed to combat a world becoming quickly disenchanted. It is a spiritual resource that opens our being to that hidden wholeness so desperately needed. It grew out of an African ground, was watered in an American environment, and has flowered in an African American religious community. That hidden wholeness can be seen, in many ways, in the black religious experience. African American religiosity is a product of its past. As we saw in chapter 2, it draws on its African roots. It has evolved into its own unique American expression.

The black religious experience has been described in many contrasting ways. It has been inadequately represented by various scholars, both European American and African American. As C. Eric Lincoln and Lawrence H. Mamiya argue: "The burden of the conventional views regarding the black Church and black religion has to do with the uncritical assumption that the black experience in religion is but the replication of the white experience, shadowed by an African patina predisposing it to an inordinate exoticism and emotionalism which distorts to a significant degree the proper expression of the faith."[43]

The black experience, in this country, is a different experience than that of many other peoples. It is shaped by tremendous suffering due to slavery, segregation, discrimination, and institutional racism. The black religiosity is, in part, the way it is because black women and men have, over the centuries, experienced God and their worship of God in the light of their continued suffering.

The black religious community came into being, in many ways, because early attempts of worship among a heterogeneous mixture of African American and European American peoples was so utterly unacceptable to whites. The majority of white religious leadership did not want to share their place and power with black congregants. The emergence and establishment of the "invisible" institutions, particularly in the South, was a liberating response among black folk in slave society. The independent black church exists because European Americans' racist attitudes and behavior provided the condition for it. They did not see themselves as equal partners in society or brothers and sisters under one Creator, God.

Peter J. Paris contends that the black church operates from within a dominant prophetic principle that can be measured within at least the two largest independent groups of black religionists—the

Methodists and the Baptists. He holds that one of the ways black religion and the black church can best be understood is in terms of a "prophetic principle of criticism."[44] The black church lives by a principle of nonracism and criticism of races in whatever form, slavery, racial segregation and discrimination. The black church "affirms the equality of all persons under God regardless of race or any other natural quality."[45] The African American church holds to a nonracist appropriation of the Christian faith, quite different from that appropriated among the significantly segregated European American church. White churches may articulate the love of one's brothers and sisters but reality illustrates a different behavior among the majority of white Christian people.

The black church, according to Paris, holds to a fundamental principle which can be described as the "biblical doctrine of the parenthood of God and the kinship of all peoples." (This is Paris's version of the more traditional and noninclusive expression "the Fatherhood of God and the brotherhood of men."[46])

In his study of *The Social Teachings of the Black Church*,[47] Paris examines the records of the black Baptist conventions and Methodist conferences to make his claim. He is particularly interested in the official motto of the African Methodist Episcopal church as it exemplifies this prophetic principle of the inclusive black church. It states that we are all one people under one God. ("God our Father, Christ our Redeemer, Man our Brother" is the traditional, noninclusive way in which the Bishops and people of the AME church have articulated that truth.) They have maintained that all of humanity is part of one race of people, the human race, and that the Christian church must first and foremost stand on that awareness. Unfortunately, the white faction of the Christian church has said one thing and done another. It has espoused a faith of brotherhood and sisterhood among all people but acted differently. The black church is the only major consistent body of believers in the United States that has remembered this basic anthropological principle. We are one race of people in the sight of God; we all are kinfolk. God is our parent, we are God's children. "God our Creator, Christ our Redeemer, Humankind our brothers and sisters" is simply another way of affirming the biblical notion of our being "people of God." We are God's people, God's children. We are brothers and sisters among the family of God.

The black religious experience represents, for Christian people within the United States, a body of people who are living out an alternative model in a world that has become more disenchanted. It is empowered by a kind of spirituality that is liberating and runs counter to many of the European American forms of religiosity.

The black church experience provides a concrete model for the larger Christian church, a model that combats the individualism, privatization, and dualism evident in our contemporary world. In its finest hours, it has provided its adherents a different and more holistic, plausible social structure in the face of often overwhelmingly oppressive conditions. The black church's basic principle of the parenthood of God and kinship of all peoples provides a context wherein believers have a greater opportunity to discover God's hidden wholeness. It is in this context that women and men, boys and girls can experience the depth of reality that God intended. This community is the African American religious community in its liberated state.

African American Ministry Models

Some examples of certain community-based ministry models, empowered in and through four predominately African American churches, will make real what we are asserting. These four congregations—an urban Christian church, an urban United Church of Christ, a rural Baptist congregation, and a United Methodist church located in the city—illustrate the creative ways in which African American religiosity and ministry practice can challenge a world often disenchanted.

The Ray of Hope Christian Church (Disciples of Christ) is pastored by the Reverend Dr. Cynthia L. Hale. This Atlanta, Georgia, congregation came into being approximately ten years ago, but presently has over one thousand members. It describes itself as a "city of hope for a people of hope." The church affirms its primary mission as one that "seeks to invite persons into relationship with

God through Jesus Christ and one another so that they can receive unconditional love and acceptance." Their stated vision is one that claims to be "a city of hope where people will impact and transform (their) present world into the [Dominion] of God."

Ray of Hope Christian Church models a kind of ministry that seeks to fulfill their mission and be directed by their vision. They provide a lay shepherding program for all members. The church advocates for an ongoing intercessory prayer ministry. Their children, youth, and young adult ministries are quite extensive. In and beyond their music ministry and other forms of Christian education, the church reaches out to those outside its doors in at least four significant ways. Ray of Hope's health ministry offers health services, education, a health fair, and long-term health-related projects for those in the community. Separate ministries for men and women are provided. Finally, their comprehensive outreach ministry provides services and affirming help to persons in the community who need their support. "Homeless, hopeless, parentless, and jobless" individuals and families are empowered through the Ray of Hope. Their goal is "to meet the needs of persons in distress by helping them help themselves; providing a cure for their situation rather than a bandage to cover their problem."[48] Ray of Hope Christian Church and its pastoral staff illustrate one of the ways in which African American spirituality is truly liberating.

Trinity United Church of Christ in Chicago, Illinois, under the leadership of the Reverend Dr. Jeremiah A. Wright Jr., is a second representative model. In March 1972, Trinity United Church of Christ adopted as its motto the phrase, "unashamedly black and unapologetically Christian." That phrase came to express a philosophy, a way of life for them. It would thereafter govern and guide that congregation and its members in all of their life together as a community of faith.

The words of that phrase have been written into the church's covenant and creed. When that covenant and creed are repeated, they "affirm in a service of public worship the congregation's ongoing attempts to remain Afrocentric in focus, worship, work, witness and program."[49]

An educational ministry is foundational to helping Trinity United live by and live out its motto. There is an emphasis on teaching

African American children their history "that they did *not* begin in slavery but in Africa before the onslaught of European (Christian) or Arab (Muslim) colonizers and slave traders, if they are to understand fully their origins or where they came from."[50]

The educational program also includes the teaching of a black value system, which includes the following tenets, among others: commitment to God; commitment to the black family; dedication to the pursuit of excellence; adherence to a black work ethic, where high productivity must be the goal of a black work force. There are also many other study programs, in addition to Bible study, using the resources of black Bible scholars like Cain Hope Felder, Charles Copher, and Randall Bailey, just to name a few.

"Service ministries that speak directly to the condition of being African American and living in the last decade of the 20th century are also ways in which we try to 'enflesh' the logos of Afrocentricity."[51] Additionally, this focus on being "unashamedly black and unapologetically Christian" is expressed through the liturgical and worship life of the church. "There is an ongoing worship design of the church (fifty-two weeks a year) which includes music and dance from the African tradition on a weekly basis; and the special African and African American observances which are celebrated by the entire church family during the regular calendar year."[52]

Powerful and effective ministries do not occur exclusively in the city. They are also present in rural settings. Valley Queen Baptist Church in Marks, Mississippi, is a good example. Dr. Carl Brown, the pastor of Valley Queen congregation, affirms this community-based church's foundational principle that "the good news of God's love is for the world." This activist Baptist church works to eliminate hunger, address economic concerns, facilitate the ministry of the laity, educate pastoral leadership, and enhance esteem for children and youth—all in the communities and select counties of rural Mississippi. The congregation attempts to feed people through worship and through nutritionally balanced meals. This congregation was the catalyst for a developing project for low-income apartment dwellers. The Quitman County (Mississippi) Development Organization (QCDO) empowers local leadership ventures. Valley Queen's pastor, Dr. Brown, has provided key leadership in this citizen-based program. These and other outreach ministries of the church provide concrete models of African American churches challenging a world supposedly disenchanted.

Finally, Glide Memorial United Methodist Church in San Francisco, California, under the activist leadership of their "minister of liberation," the Reverend Cecil Williams, presents another model of community-based ministry. This extraordinary church has for years reached out to its community and beyond. Crack addicts discover recovery, abused women come to themselves through a healing process, abusive men are empowered to release their rage.[53] This inner-city church offers itself to the masses in the so-called Tenderloin district of San Francisco. It provides transformation of individuals and whole groups of persons. It has established a national network of African American churches fighting the crack cocaine epidemic. This nationally known church and pastor have one primary mission. It is a mission that calls for an attack "against addiction and for the empowerment of the African American family." Its pastor, Cecil Williams, "envisions a society in which there is no need to hide, one in which we recognize our problems, define ourselves, feel our pain, tell our truths, and come together in a community that accepts us as we are and nurtures us to wholeness and health."[54] Glide Memorial United Methodist Church shows us what it means to act like and be a church involved in a liberating spirituality.

This chapter has attempted to describe the present reality of our social existence, especially in the United States. We assert that human beings still treat one another differently with regard to class, race, and gender. We are living in a racist society, a world that is divided by financial resources, and one that evaluates persons in terms of their being male or female. Below that stark and oppressive reality lies a deeper fundamental concern—we are losing an awareness of the mystery and comprehensive depth of God's creation. We are on the road to becoming a world disenchanted. Yet, we gravitate toward the hope that God will show us a way back and forward toward God's intended design. God provided a way for men and women who went through the "desert experience" of slavery. God, we trust, will show us a way again.

After you explore the following questions for reflection and action, we invite you to explore the ways in which our lives are interconnected (chapter 4).

Questions for Reflection and Action

1. In what ways could our life today be described as "dis howlin' wildaness?" What special groups of people in our society may use these ideas to express their reality? How can you, as an individual and along with others, begin to effect change?

2. It is commonly thought in the United States that freedom and justice are individually based ideals. Do you agree or disagree? Develop a position in support of or in opposition to that statement.

3. Recall a sermon that you have heard recently, perhaps last Sunday. State ways in which the biblical message was related to life situations—personal, communal, and in the world.

4. Pause to envision and evaluate the human condition today in our world, our nation, your county, or your city. What are some things that excite you? that make you feel good? that distress you? How do they leave your spirit? In what ways are you and others working to make a difference?

5. What opportunities exist in your congregation or institution to explore the deep questions about faith commitment and the pain and suffering of persons in today's world? What are some significant responses and decisions that result from such mutual reflection?

6. Study the biblical passage: Isaiah 35. Note verse 1: Are there desert places in your city, your county, our nation, and in our world? How is Isaiah's vision of restoration and transformation being realized in those situations that you know? What could be done that is not being done? And what can you, alone or with others, do to effect change?

4

"In a Single Garment of Destiny"
Our Life Together

All this is simply to say that all life is interrelated. We are
caught in an inescapable network of mutuality; tied in a single
garment of destiny. Whatever affects one directly, affects all indirectly. . . . This is the way the world is made. I didn't make
it that way, but this is the interrelated structure of reality. [1]

Some writers like Thomas Merton, Paul Tillich, Reinhold Niebuhr,
Mahatma Gandhi, Howard Thurman, Martin Luther King Jr.,
Matthew Fox, Rosemary Ruether, and Letty Russell see the solution
of world problems such as racism, sexism, classism, and the ecological crisis in a holistic way; that is, they view these problems from
a global perspective. These gifted individuals reflect on specific
world issues while seeing the relationship among them.

For instance, when Martin Luther King Jr. gave the commence-
ment address at Lincoln University in Pennsylvania on June 6, 1961,
he said that for the American public to realize "The American
Dream," the first thing to affirm is that the dream is universal, the
dream comes out of the struggles of all persons. He further declared
that each person has certain basic rights that are conferred by the
states.

King said, however, that the United States professes a balance between the whole and the individual, yet practices the exact opposite.
He affirmed that American society has a "schizophrenic personality." The Nobel laureate stated that while our scientific genius and

research may have made us a world community or neighborhood, we must open ourselves to a spiritual reality that surrounds us in order to regain a truly interconnected society.

King helps us with such a global perspective by writing of mutuality, interrelatedness, or the assertion that we are "tied in a single garment of destiny." In 1963 King expanded on "The American Dream" theme by stating in Washington, D.C. on August 28, 1963:

> I say to you today, my friends, though, even though we face the difficulties of today and tomorrow, I still have a dream. It is a dream deeply rooted in the American dream. I have a dream that one day this nation will rise up, live out the true meaning of its creed: "We hold these truths to be self-evident, that all men are created equal."
>
> I have a dream that one day on the red hills of Georgia sons of former slaves and the sons of former slave-owners will be able to sit down together at the table of brotherhood. I have a dream that one day even the state of Mississippi, a state sweltering with the heat of injustice, sweltering with the heat of oppression, will be transformed into an oasis of freedom and justice.
>
> I have a dream that my four little children will one day live in a nation where they will not be judged by the color of their skin but by the content of their character. I have a dream . . . I have a dream that one day in Alabama, with its vicious racists, with its governor having his lips dripping with the words of interposition and nullification, one day right there in Alabama little black boys and black girls will be able to join hands with little white boys and white girls as sisters and brothers.
>
> I have a dream today . . . I have a dream that one day every valley shall be exalted, every hill and mountain shall be made low. The rough places will be made plain, and the crooked places will be made straight. And the glory of [God] shall be revealed, and all flesh shall see it together. This is our hope. This is the faith that I go back to the South with. With this faith we will be able to hew out of the mountain of despair a stone of hope. With this faith we will be able to transform the jangling discords of our nation into a beautiful symphony of [kinship]. With this faith we will be able to work together, to stand up for freedom together, knowing that we will be free one day.[2]

Martin Luther King pointed us to a fundamental reality of our existence: We are not alone—and more than that, we are all in this together.

Interconnected and Not Alone

We are individual selves but certainly not self-autonomous individuals. How we connect with one another, in the same city much less
across the globe, is often a complex matter. But we are connected,
even interconnected. As Martin Luther King affirms, "whatever affects one directly, affects all indirectly." The weather in one part of
the world eventually influences weather in another. The products we
import and export are distributed around the world. Our agricul-
tural policies influence the amounts of grain we grow and export.
That in turn affects the levels of grain available to those who need
food. The coffee grown for export in Ghana, West Africa, in place
of food for Ghana's people, contributes to the impoverishment of
Ghana's masses. This is the case in most countries of our world. We
are interconnected as nations, through our world economic and government policies. We are interconnected in other ways.

Our advanced means of mass communication have enabled us to
observe and witness the varying ways we live and move about in our
contemporary settings. Cable News Network and other resources
function as a means to see, hear, and feel somewhat the actions and
thoughts of most people on our planet. It was estimated that approximately 60 percent of the world's population observed, in some
fashion, the 1996 Atlanta Olympic games. We are a people who are
becoming daily more aware of one another.

With this awareness, our lives are becoming more inter-
twined. Thus, externally, through resource distribution and in-
ternally through values, customs, and norms displayed, we are
not isolated and private individuals but members of a global family.
"We Are Family," as the 1970s popular song goes—more today than
ever before.

And yet our fears of others across town, as well as those who
sound and look significantly different across the globe, motivate us

too often to withdraw into our own subgroups or plausibility structures. We seek homogeneous enclaves for protection instead of enjoying an interconnected richness of existence. We seek sanctuary and supposed sameness because we fear change and others who appear to be a threat. Our fears too often motivate us instead of our love. As Henri Nouwen says, we appear to be fundamentally "fearful people." "The more people I come to know and the more I come to know people, the more I am overwhelmed by the negative power of fear. It often seems that fear has invaded every part of our being to such a degree that we no longer know what a life without fear would feel like."[3]

There are sufficient reasons to be fearful in our contemporary context. Nuclear weapons still exist in this country and others. The creative ways we have continued to pollute our air, water, and soil persist. Wars, terrorism, and mass murder observed in the former Yugoslavia and Rwanda endure. Human beings, when exercising power over other human communities, can too easily destroy life instead of sustaining it. Adults and children commit unthinkable crimes against one another. Human life, especially that of black people, seems cheap today. Excessive substance abuse seems symptomatic of our internal and external decay. We have valid reasons for angst and fear. The complexity of our communities, cities, nation, and world seems overwhelming at times. When we allow ourselves to see ourselves as private, individual entities in the midst of a multilayered and pluralistic world context, we cannot help but feel frustrated.

But we are not private, individual, and isolated people. We are more than an *I;* we are a *we.* And a more holistic perspective is required if we are going to be active participants in a liberating spirituality that dispels this fearful isolationism. Part of the hidden wholeness that needs to be revealed, thus less hidden, is one that negates our segmented and privatized self-understandings. We must see ourselves and others as parts of a greater whole. We are unique persons of individuality, but participants in a larger context.

Cornel West uses the metaphor of jazz, not as "a musical art form," but for "a mode of being in the world," to illustrate our interconnectedness and communal interdependence.

The interplay of individuality and unity is not one of uniformity and unanimity imposed from above, but rather of conflict among diverse groupings that reach a dynamic consensus subject to questioning and criticism. As with a soloist in a jazz quartet, quintet or band, individuality is promoted in order to sustain and increase the *creative* tension with the group—a tension that yields higher levels of performance to achieve the aim of the collective project.[4]

The goal of building a cooperative and interconnected community and global family is assumed in a liberating spirituality. It is a spirituality that affirms the one Sovereign God who created us to live our lives in relationship and not in fear-driven competition. Ours is a God who calls us to discover or rediscover that wholeness, while at times still hidden, that can empower us to "achieve the aim of the collective project."

The Individual and Society

To effectively discern God's will and call, one that supports a healthy individuality within the community/society, one must affirm a more holistic perspective in terms of our contemporary society. Andrew Billingsley has developed a comprehensive understanding of the self and its connectedness with the greater society. It is important, Billingsley implies, that we see the fluidity of movement among the individual, family, community, and larger North American society. The individual child and children relate to the world through families (nuclear, extended, and augmented) and other key mediating structures in the community (churches, schools, businesses, and other voluntary associations). These intermediate associations, such as Christian churches, character-building schools, Muslim mosques, fraternities/sororities, etc., enable the individual child and adult to relate to the larger world. There are many significant societal systems that impact, positively and negatively, these community-based associations, and thus influence the family and individual person. Billingsley identifies multiple systems in our society that influence individuals and families. They involve parts of government, private businesses, voluntary (that are nonsectarian), and religious sectors of our society. They both influence and are influenced by the individual, her family, his church, her school, etc. They are—we are—related. We live in a dynamic, mutually interconnected society. This is the reality of our contemporary existence.[5]

The creative or liberating ways in which we have maneuvered existence in the midst of these influencing and influenceable sectors of our reality is important to remember. It is especially important as we attempt to discover or rediscover a spirituality that opens us to a hidden wholeness.

We argue that the communities, churches, schools, and families have been and will continue to be the primary sources or mediating structures for a liberating spirituality so necessary today. These intermediate institutions or associations are the major means available to the individual attempting to make sense of his or her social existence within our complex society and world. This has been profoundly so for African Americans. These "intermediate institutions that affirm the humanity of black people, accent their capacities and potentialities, and foster the character and excellence requisite for productive citizenship, are beacons of hope in the midst of the cultural and moral crisis."[6] The community and communities, churches, schools, and families have served as the primary bulwark against systemic and negative influences on African Americans—historically and at present. As the following diagram attempts to convey, these primary social entities (the community, church, school, and family) are primary sources for revealing the hidden wholeness of human existence. They provide an intermediate means of living a liberated existence in the midst of a hostile society. They nurture a potentially joyous spirituality in a racist world context. They are the important mediating structures of social existence that birth, incubate, and sustain black life in an oppressive existence.

Anne Wimberly, one of our faculty colleagues, has observed firsthand the differences between the dominant Eurocentric culture and African American culture seminary experience. In reflecting on her move from a predominately white seminary to Interdenominational Theological Center (ITC), whose population is mostly black, she could compare and contrast the two settings. At ITC the cultural emphasis is one of community and inclusiveness. Wimberly said: "Here we embrace one another irrespective of place in the commu-

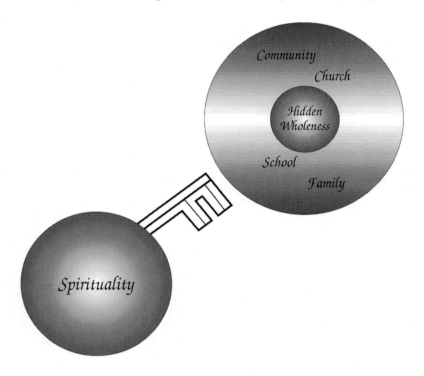

nity. There is a freedom in relationship among students, staff, professors, deans, the President, housekeeping and maintenance. We are 'together' in this place and experience. There is no meeting and shying away, but rather real encounter."[7]

In reflecting on the community response to a death in the family of a faculty colleague, Wimberly witnessed the strengths of African American spirituality:

> When the late Tom Pugh's first wife, Lillian, died there was the reaching out of the community to him, as is noted in other similar communities. The difference was evidenced in the other aspects very common, spontaneous and unrehearsed in African American culture. The "eye contact," the "touching," the "greeting" are all characteristics that are found here at ITC on a consistent basis, whereas, they are not so often found in predominately white seminaries. These qualities permeate every location

and event and time in our seminary experience. Caring is not neat and clinical, as appears to be the case in white institutions.[8]

The African American Community— A Place to Start

Among many in American society, the starting point of awareness is the isolated individual or family. This is not the case generally in the black community. The African American community, in many ways, communicates to its members that the community is the starting place, not the private or isolated individual. The feeling or sense of a greater whole is expressed in and through the black community. This quality or sense of community origin comes from African culture and is carried over today beyond indigenous African society.

John Mbiti underscores that throughout traditional African cultures there is a deep sense of community. The individual is born into a tribe and family, but sees him/herself as more than an individual self or creature. He or she is part of a larger whole—the community. The person becomes who he or she is in community and not as distinct from it. "In traditional life, the individual does not and cannot exist alone except corporately," Mbiti explains. Individuals owe their existence to others, including members of past generations as well contemporaries. They are "simply part of the whole."

> The community must therefore make, create or produce the individual; for the individual depends on that corporate group. Physical birth is not enough: the child must go through rites of incorporation so that it becomes fully integrated into the entire society. The rites continue throughout the physical life of the person, during which the individual passes from one stage of corporate existence to another. The final stage is reached when he [or she] dies and even then he [or she] is ritually incorporated into the wider family of both the dead and the living.[9]

Mbiti affirms that this understanding of the human creature is profoundly religious in traditional African culture. God made the first human being and now humans produce others, but others who become corporate or social beings. This, according to Mbiti, is a "deeply religious transaction." He explains that only in terms of others do individuals become conscious of their own being, their own duties, privileges, and responsibilities toward themselves and others. When individuals suffer, they do so "not alone but with the corporate group"; when individuals rejoice, they do so "not alone but with . . . relatives dead or living." When a person marries, he or she is not alone, nor does he or she have any ownership claim on the spouse.

> So also the children belong to the corporate body of kin[folk], even if they bear only their father's name. Whatever happens to the individual happens to the whole group, and whatever happens to the whole group happens to the individual. The individual can only say: "I am, because we are; and since we are, therefore I am." This is a cardinal point in the understanding of the African view of [humankind].[10]

It is a view that is consistent with an underlying principle of Christian experience, wherein members of the body of Christ belong to one another. The apostle Paul proposes that this is the nature of the Christian community, "for we are members of one another" (Eph. 4:25b). The letter to the church at Corinth makes the same point. "If one member suffers, all suffer together with it; if one member is honored, all rejoice together with it" (1 Cor. 12:26).

Again, the African American community has found a way to maintain this basic African and early Christian belief system. The basic community and those community ties which exist among its individual members are of primary importance. People are connected to one another within the framework of the larger community. Individual contractual relations are important but experienced within a deeper sense of community. Communal bonds among black men and women appear stronger than any other group in the United States. These socioreligious group ties are a significant indicator of the importance of community in the African American context.

All communities are social systems. They are organized entities. All communities have certain guiding values and norms. All communities have key institutions that reinforce these norms, sentiments and expectations. No single community is completely uniform, all have diversity within them. But most all communities have members that hold fairly consistent and commonly shared goals and values. Such is the case in the African American community.

Andrew Billingsley affirms the significant presence of the black community, that it most certainly exists, and does so in both weak and strong ways.

> Even as it is undergoing constant change, major generative elements endure. The community is capable of providing resources and assistance. Any community composed of 30 million people, most of whom live in families, most of whom are no longer poor, with combined annual income exceeding $300 billion, more than 400,000 black-owned business firms, some 75,000 black-owned churches, a hundred black colleges, and numerous other organizations, with a common history, common identity, and successful struggles against the adversities of life, cannot be reasonably defined as impotent.[11]

Billingsley goes on to highlight the unique aspects of the African American community in four specific ways. The black community, for the most part, shares a common geographical location. Most families and individuals live in neighborhoods that are overwhelmingly populated by black persons. This is often the case because of economic factors and racist policies that reinforce this reality. But whatever the reasons, black folk live together in most geographical settings.[12]

Second, the African American community is defined by its shared set of values, goals, and norms. These centrally held values and beliefs were maintained in the past and held today, even in the presence of great difficulty. The importance of the family, the commitment to hard work, the supreme value of education, and the necessity of individual initiative are values honored in the black community. They are community-based and consensus-built sentiments that the majority of African American people share.[13]

Third, most black women and men live their lives grounded in an appreciation for and commitment to their heritage. They remember who they are and where they have come from. They claim their past and reaffirm over and over again their history. They feel connected to those who have gone before them and "made a way" for those who follow.

Finally, Billingsley argues that the African American community maintains its geographical ties, core values, and proud heritage through a set of specific institutions and organizations which serve primarily black families and people. He groups these organizations into four overall entities: "the church, the school, the business enterprise, and the voluntary organization."[14] We have chosen to focus on only two of these four community-based entities: the black church and school. If the black community is the place to start, the church represents the place to be.

The African American Church—A Place to Be

It is important to remember that any discussion of black existence in American society must include a discussion of the African American church. The church is the primary institution in the black community. It is at its center. In fact, it is often difficult to distinguish between the black church and the black community. They are inextricably interwoven. Lincoln makes this observation.

> To understand the power of the black Church, it must first be understood that there is no disjunction between the black Church and the black community. The church is the spiritual face of the black subculture, and whether one is a "church member" or not is beside the point. Because of the singular nature of the black experience and the centrality of institutionalized religion in the development of that experience, the credentials of personal identity, in times not too far past, depended primarily upon church affiliation. Thus, to belong to "Mt. Nebo Baptist" or to go to "Mason's Chapel Methodist" was the accepted way of establishing who one was and how [one] was to be regarded in the community.[15]

Thus the term "black religious community" includes both the African American church and the larger community. That community exists, in large part, by the life blood of its center—the black church.

The African American church has many strengths, some of which can be measured quantitatively.

> Based on the indices of church membership, church atten-
> dance, and charitable giving in 1987, different studies have
> pointed out the following: about 78 percent of the black pop-
> ulation claimed church membership and attended once in the
> last six months; blacks (44 percent) tend to have slightly higher
> rates of weekly church attendance than white Protestants (40
> percent); and they have the highest rates of being super-
> churched (attending church more than on Sundays) among all
> Americans (37 versus 31 percent). The seven major black de-
> nominations have not suffered the kind of severe decline in
> membership experienced by some mainstream white denomi-
> nations like the Discipleship of Christ (40 percent), the United
> Presbyterian church (33 percent), or the Episcopal church (33
> percent).[16]

Beyond these quantitative indices of the strength of the black church, there are certain qualitative elements that are important. There are specific qualities of the black religious world that are present and are sorely needed among adherents of the broader Christian community. The African American religious worldview offers some healthy alternatives in the face of many of the societal problems highlighted in the previous chapter.

The source of these qualities is found in African and African American culture. They differ, obviously, from a European American perspective, the dominant worldview in the United States. Instead of a competitive individualism, a cooperative collectivism is encountered in the black church. A sense of community and connectedness is discovered in the religious community of the black world. Personal worth and self-esteem based on helping others is seen within the African American context, rather than an individual's worth being predicated on his or her own acquisition and possessive of material wealth. In the face of assumed racial superiority, the black religious world advocates racial parity, inclusion, and freedom.

The authors dare to claim that while the African American religious community and its worldview are neither perfect nor uniformly consistent, they do offer a healthy alternative to many of the problems we face in this country. That worldview is driven by certain attractive values that differ from some of the destructive ones so indicated in this book. It is a black religious community worldview that is needed, especially as we, in the Christian church, attempt to challenge some of our fundamental problems: economic injustice, racism, and sexism. The African American religious context offers important elements that can help us claim our needed self-understanding. The black church exhibits ingredients of what it means to be the "people of God" in the world. Cooperative collectivism, a sense of community, self-worth based on helping others, and a nonracist Christian faith are only four indicators of this self-understanding.

The black community, like other social communities, has key institutions and organizations. The African American church is obviously a primary one. It embodies all four ingredients of the black community highlighted earlier in this chapter: geographical location, strongly held values, identity-based heritage, and organizational life. The black community, for African American people, is the place to start. The church is the place to be. The school, another key institution in black community life, is the place to grow.

The African American School— A Place to Grow

Education is of utmost importance in the black community. A fundamental belief in education has driven African American mothers and fathers for years. Billingsley explains, "For more than a hundred years, each generation of blacks has been more educated than the one before. This has been reflected in every area of education, including basic literacy, school attendance, highest grade level achieved, and percentage going on to and graduating college and beyond."[17] Education has played a preeminent role in the life of the African American community. This has always been the case.

The desire to read and write and learn was prevalent among African Americans in antebellum America. This thirst for learning, "crossed the Atlantic with the African captives."[18] Their hunger for education was "well developed in the era of the African Renaissance which spread to the West African coast, that even slavery could not quench it."[19]

It is interesting to note that much of the educational enterprise in the South resulted from New England philanthropy. As Lincoln suggests: "Deep in the pragmatics of the Yankee mentality was the firm conviction that education was the only key capable of unlocking Africans' potential for the mature religious understanding which could in time prepare them for responsible moral behavior and political responsibility."[20] Black folk have continued to seize opportunities for education aggressively. They have turned education to advantage in a move for self-development and self-improvement.

Billingsley cites the following statistics. Shortly after the period of slavery, in 1890, one-third of all African American children under the age of twenty-one were attending schools. By 1910 roughly 45 percent of black children were enrolled in school, increasing to 65 percent by 1940. In 1975 the percentage of black children in school was approximately the same as white children, roughly 87 percent.[21] These figures illustrate the significance and great value of education in the black community. After hundreds of years of oppression, slavery, and devaluation, African American fathers and mothers taught their children to believe in and seek higher education.

Between 1830 and 1900 the value of a college education increased, in the African American experience, with the creation of the historically black colleges. Today, over 140 traditional black colleges exist, educating masses of young black women and men. The majority of these schools are located in the southern part of the United States, and remain the school of choice for "some two hundred thousand black students."[22] As C. Eric Lincoln affirms: "More than any other institution, the black college has provided a solid affirmation for black identity, freeing the battered black ego from the nagging doubts which are the inevitable corollaries of a total life experience washed in denigration and constraint."[23]

The drive for education in every conceivable form, at every level of schooling, has motivated black men and women for years. In part, this motivation grew out of the stark reality that mainstream institutions were closed to black people—until recent years. But more importantly, African American leadership has always preferred and

valued the "ownership, control and protection of their cultural heritage,"[24] which the traditional black schools have provided. African
American colleges, universities, and theological seminaries have existed and exist today to educate black women and men to the reality of their existence. Nowhere else, other than the church, can black
persons grow to appreciate their African heritage, African American
culture, and black identity than in these long-established institutions. These schools continue to provide excellent role models for
black youth and produce "creditable numbers" of scholars, scientists, political leaders, and clergy "whose contributions to America
and the world are eloquent argument for their respectability."[25]

The purpose of training men and women for effective ministry in
the black community and greater society is a part of the mission of
the Interdenominational Theological Center (ITC). While this is the
educational setting within which we are teaching and writing this
book, it represents, in most ways, the many black schools that exist
across this country. The ITC, like other African American institutions of higher learning, have several objectives that are unique to
the black experience.

ITC is located in the heart of one of the largest centers for black
education in the world. It, like the other five educational institutions
(Clark Atlanta University, Morehouse College, Morehouse School
of Medicine, Morris Brown College, and Spelman College) that
make up the Atlanta University Center complex, seeks to educate
women and men for service in the community and world. That service may vary in terms of profession, but it is service nonetheless.

An appreciation for African and African American history, culture, and experience is paramount in the black school. Support for
the ongoing struggle for the liberation of oppressed peoples in the
United States and beyond is critical. A critique of European American history, culture, and experience in light of the African and
African American context is also present in the black educational
environment. Thus, service in the church and society (an ITC goal)
or service through other professions (a goal of black colleges in general) in the community and world is encouraged in correlation with
the African American worldview and ethos.

These invaluable institutions of higher learning enable black men
and women to experience a liberating spirituality in the midst of a

larger oppressive and negating society. They help young people and those seeking second and third career opportunities the chance to grow as persons and participants in the broader community. The school, in the African American community, is essential. "Education is the traditional opportunity through which black families find their places in life. And having found it, they replicate their experiences again and again through their children."[26]

The African American Family—
A Place to Live

If the black school is a place to grow, the African American family provides the primary place to live. The family, extended and otherwise, is the fundamental social unit in the black community. It is *the* intimate association that provides life and breath for the children of the African American world. Children are at the center of black family life and nurtured by the other key societal components highlighted in this chapter—the broader community, the church, and the school. In fact, the real test of how well families function may have more to do with their dependents than almost any other factor. If those dependents—the boys and girls that exist within the nuclear and extended families of the community—fare well, the family can be said to be on solid ground.

A myth developed in more recent years is one that has characterized the black family as being synonymous with one type of family grouping—an African American unwed teenage mother and child or children. This myth, perpetuated by the media and others, has developed around single parents. The truth is that most single parents are not teenagers but adults, and most are not black but white. This is certainly not the picture we receive in most discussions concerning the black family.

The African American family, similar to other ethnic groupings in the United States, is diverse in its structure. There are family units that are headed by single persons, cohabitants, individuals who are married but without children, persons with children but not married, those married and having children, children living with grandparents, blended families, augmented ones, etc. The family structure in the black community is as diverse as any other. It, like all families in our country, influences and is influenced by those immediate community social institutions (churches, schools, business enterprises, and voluntary associations) and the larger society which makes up the government, private business, voluntary and religious sectors.

In the African American experience, the concept of extended family is readily affirmed. It is manifested in many ways. One persistent expression is that of family reunions, which gather individuals and groups from far and near with some regularity. While other ethnic groupings in our society value family gatherings, the importance of the extended family continues to be essential in the black community. The heritage of African Americans is such that the larger understanding of family supersedes the primary "nuclear" emphasis so dominant in American society.

The so-called crisis of the family, which we hear articulated with great regularity by our politicians, comes from many influencing social factors. Domestic violence, poverty, marital conflicts, stress, substance abuse, unemployment, divorce, and school failure are but a few of the forces impacting all families, including the African American family. How the family responds to these problems is of utmost importance. The black family has responded amazingly well. What it has been able to do, against all odds, speaks well of the black family unit.

People of African heritage have had and continue to have family life characteristics that support them during the worse of times. African people, brought to this country against their will, brought with them certain liberating codes of conduct which sustained them during the humiliation and devastation of the slave trade period.

Scholars, in more recent years, have verified critical family codes and family patterns that slave men and women would have participated in prior to their dehumanizing abduction from parts of Africa. For example, ancient Egyptians or Kemets significantly contributed to world civilization in terms of family life patterns, as did other Nile Valley civilizations. Key roles for men and women, the value of marriage, the great importance of children, strong emphasis on the love and honoring of one another, etc., were important family codes of behavior in so-called ancient days. The scholarship of Asa Hilliard,

Charles S. Finch, Cheikh Anta Diop, Martin Bernal, Ivan Van Sertima, Yosef ben-Jochannan, and others has given us greater clarity in terms of African contributions to world civilization.[27]

As African men and women moved out from the Nile Valley areas to other parts of the continent, like West Africa, they carried with them these family characteristics. Again, scholarship has uncovered a great deal of evidence that suggests that family patterns, developed among the African diaspora, survived the American experience. They may have been "diluted and transformed by it but not destroyed."[28] Several key components of family life survived: relationships based more on blood ties than any others, extended family life, the central impact of children, role reciprocity, etc. The point to note here is that African American families have had a long historical heritage to draw on as they have attempted to survive and flourish on American soil. African men and women were brought to this country as individual slaves but arrived with a collective memory and experience of family life that would sustain them against all odds. There is significant evidence from slave narratives and other sources that demonstrate that "neither the idea nor the experience of family was obliterated by slavery. Instead, the family was re-created and reconstructed based on the family ideas, values, and yearnings the Africans brought with them in their memories and sustained through the harsh realities of slave life in European-oriented North America."[29] The centrality of the mother, the extended-family idea, and the remarkable way that families learned how to be flexible, resilient, and adaptive are distinctive aspects of the African American family. These formidable family-life traits have helped the black community and its people to more than make it in Western culture. They have given the community its life blood.

Today, the African American community nurtures its families with key traditional family values that sustain its men, women, boys, and girls. These values concerning spirituality, self-help, self-governance, service to others, cooperation with others, racial pride, and black private enterprise are fundamentally present in our American scene.[30] The black family is a part of a community that is neither dead nor dying, but is generative in its internal and external resources. It is a community that has a great many strengths. These individual strengths and collective gifts are spiritual, intellectual, cultural, social, physical, economic and political. Their manifestation can be seen in tremendous advances made in education; the movement from working class to the middle class; the significant increase of the African American business class; the varied and rich contribution of persons in science, medicine, technology and the arts. The list could be continued. The truth is the family has been and continues to be a critical place to sustain generative black life in the United States. It is the mediating structure or environment which provides *the* place to live for African American people.

The church, school, and family in the larger African American community have provided settings for protection, growth, and empowerment for years. The community was and is the place of origin, the place to start. Living not as individual and isolated selves but as members of a greater whole—this is the African American experience. The church is the place to be, a context to discover and claim one's deepest reality. A place to encounter God, reflect on that encounter, and prepare to act according to God's way in the world— this is the reality we call "church." And finally, the family—the place to live—is the haven to raise children, transmit values and goals, and protect and prepare oneself to act in the world.

These three social institutions—the family, school, and church— are key ingredients to black community life. They are interdependent parts of a greater whole. They support the fabric that makes up our single garment of destiny.

Leadership and a Liberating Spirituality

The African American community and its mediating structures of church, school, and family have been empowered through continuous liberated leadership. Leadership drawn from the religious world of the black community has always been and continues to be of primary importance. Leadership that provides a liberating spirituality often has been essential in the black struggle with American life and its many contextual challenges. Strong spiritual leadership has emerged from within the African American world when it was desperately needed. This has always been the case.

Women and men have responded positively to the call of God,

over the years, when the African American community and church needed effective, spiritually liberating leadership. Phillis Wheatley, Jarena Lee, Rebecca Cox Jackson, Amanda Berry Smith, Maria W. Stewart, Harriet Tubman, Sojourner Truth, Frances Jackson Coppin, Dr. Anna Julia Cooper, Dr. Mary McLeod Bethune, Nannie Helen Burroughs, Ella Baker, and Fannie Lou Hamer are but a few women in history who, in their own unique ways, provided leadership when it was needed. The number of men who have offered themselves, through the empowering presence of God to the black community and larger society, is significant. To name only a few from the past, we would include Henry Highland Garnett, Andrew Bryan, Richard Allen, Absalom Jones, Martin R. Delany, Alexander Crummell, Henry McNeal Turner, Marcus Garvey, Charles H. Mason, Elijah Muhammad, Martin Luther King Jr., and Malcolm X. These individuals possessed different gifts and thus provided varying forms of leadership in different historical contexts. But leadership—an empowering kind, grounded in a liberating spirituality—emerged in these and other women and men over the past centuries. The African American community, its churches, schools, and various families today would not be what they are without strong and effective leadership.

Some would argue that American society, and particularly the African American community, lacks the kind of moral leadership we have seen in the recent past in persons like Martin Luther King Jr., Malcolm X, Ella Baker, and Fannie Lou Hamer. The crisis of black leadership is articulated by some scholars at present, particularly black political and intellectual leadership. Cornel West argues that today the kind of leadership modeled by persons such as Adam Clayton Powell Jr., Ronald Dellums, and James Baldwin is not as evident. With the possible exceptions of Jesse Jackson in the political realm and Toni Morrison in the intellectual, "the present generation has yet to produce such a figure,"[31] West asserts.

West argues that there is a crisis of leadership because of several factors. A "relative lack of authentic anger," coupled with a "relative absence of genuine humility," he sees as missing among most contemporary leadership.[32] Too few persons provide leadership that challenges both us and our institutions, with an urgency about the state of black America. Too few give public and private evidence of the "common touch and humble disposition toward ordinary black people,"[33] West proposes. He suggests that most black scholars, like their white counterparts, are mere academicians, "narrowly confined to specialized disciplines with little sense of broader life of the mind and hardly any engagement with battles in the streets."[34] The quality of leadership is lessening, he argues, because the "personal, familial and communal relations among African Americans"[35] have been bombarded with overwhelming social crises—some of which we have highlighted in this and the previous chapter. Racism, economic injustice, and sexism greatly influence black life in America. Poverty, homelessness, substance abuse, marital conflict, and unemployment significantly impact the African American individual, family, and larger community. Thus, West would argue, the natural place to foster charismatic leadership—the black community—is today experiencing such a nihilistic threat that it does so less than in years past. The communal resources needed to help African American men and women cope with reality, and at the same time give birth to and nurture new effective leadership, seem to be waning.

Whether this is true in the latter part of the 1990s is questionable. While we believe that West, at times, overstates the case with generalities concerning black life in America, his point is worth considering. New and fresh leadership is needed in our country. We argue that that leadership has been, and must continue to be, a kind that models a liberating spirituality. It is a necessary challenge for our times. To use West's categories, it is leadership that is "humble" because it is grounded in an encounter with the source of our being—God. It is "angry" or urgent because that encounter and spiritual reflection have moved leadership to a liberating and assertive action in the world. Men and women who have arrived on the battlefield to lead God's army against injustice must do so with a word from God. There is no other way to provide genuine leadership which truly motivates people to a liberating awareness and action. This is a God-directed initiative. It is a process that must be grounded in the center of our individual and collective reality. It is what lies behind and beneath that which we call our hidden wholeness.

Spirituality, as we have claimed in this text, is not a "warm and fuzzy" kind of experience. It is a powerful and empowering process—one that involves us in a liberating encounter, liberating reflection, and a liberating action. Spirituality involves the whole person, within the whole community of faith, with the whole of life. We are not dualistic creatures: body and soul, inhabitants of heaven and earth, separated by good and evil. We are whole people, experiencing all of life, in the whole of existence. Our spirituality reinforces a connectedness that integrates the totality of existence.

Relevant leadership in our society, communities, and churches must be grounded in this encompassing spirituality. Those of us within the Judeo-Christian tradition claim that this leadership is such as it is because it is based on our relationship with God in Jesus Christ. We celebrate a God who revealed the Divine Self, in a particular person among a particular people at a particular time in history. We follow Jesus of Nazareth. We affirm his life, death, and resurrection. There are many ways God has and continues to reveal the Divine Self, but our particular experience is one that is grounded in the greater Christian story.

Leadership that emerges from a liberating spirituality begins with God's call and an affirming response. Spiritual leadership has to do with vocation or *Kaléo* ("to call"). We are called by God, into the world *to be* (encounter/reflection) and *to do* (action) something specific for and with God. Our leadership is more than an occupation, a career, or a job. It is a calling. Henri Nouwen reminds us that "career and vocation are not mutually exclusive. In fact, our vocation might require us to pursue a certain career. Many people have become excellent doctors, lawyers, technicians, or scientists in response to God's call heard in the community."[36] Understanding this claim of God on one's life and affirming that our separate gifts, talents, and skills are to be offered in service for our common life enables us to discover the hidden wholeness.

God is already there and here—in the world. God is present, acting in God's way, in our society. God invites us to join God in God's transforming presence and activity. God is liberating people and communities. We are called to participate with God in this liberating movement.

Some essential characteristics of this leadership—a leadership that represents a liberating spirituality—are ones we have witnessed in our students and colleagues, as well as persons beyond our ministry settings. These qualities or attributes, when present in the lives of men and women who provide spiritual leadership, give those whom they would lead a greater opportunity of experiencing liberation. These characteristics are related to servanthood, being good listeners, leading people, displaying integrity, and practicing what we preach.

Servant Leadership

The Reverend Dr. Gerald Durley, a recent visitor to our campus, said we too often desire "eaglehood instead of servanthood." Leaders sometimes desire the admiration of others to the degree that they take themselves too seriously. They need to remember, as an African proverb states: "It takes more than one head to arrive at a decision." Either arrogance or low self-esteem can inflate our idea of ourselves. We are called by God to serve others. Jesus modeled this kind of servant leadership when he voluntarily washed the feet of his disciples. We must take God's call seriously. We must be serious about the ministry of the church. However, we need to take ourselves less seriously!

To be in front of people, center stage, is a condition that often seduces us into thinking that we are more important that we really are. Empowering spiritual leadership usually calls for servanthood among its advocates.

Being a Good Listener

Listening to others is critical for a kind of liberating spirituality and leadership. Being truly present to the other is a gift to the other. In our experiences, too many clergy and lay leaders today are better talkers than they are listeners. Being anxious, afraid, wanting to better the other's story, or simply being interested in one's primary agenda are all sources of inadequate listening. Being spiritually grounded, being centered in the active presence of God can and will enable us to be present to those who respond to our leadership. Listening with our whole being to individuals and groups of persons is a necessary component of liberating leadership.

Spiritual Leadership

Leading people instead of attempting to rule over them is another important characteristic. There is a significant difference between spiritual leadership and group dictatorship. The communities we live in don't need passive, confused, or indecisive leaders. Nor do they require despots. Leadership can be authoritative without being authoritarian.

Leadership has to be shared. Decision making ought to be more democratic and participatory. Our lives and our communities are threatened by many evil forces in our society. Therefore, more than ever before, we need decisive leadership. However, if we offer a liberating mode of leadership, we will learn to lead others without attempting to govern them.

Pastoral leadership in the African American church setting has always been essential. Historically, the pastor has been the central, authoritative figure. While we do not advocate a diminution of the pastoral role, we do affirm the need for shared, participatory leadership. Many lay women and men, in the contemporary church, are equipped to share in congregational and communitywide leadership. The world and our society's problems are too formidable to ignore valuable lay leadership. Together, in a shared form of leadership, the needs of the church and the community can be addressed more effectively.

Personal Integrity

Integrity is so important. Our media resources communicate the failings of our contemporary leadership enthusiastically. Being an honest, genuine leader is vital in our society. People will follow spiritually liberated men and women if they live lives worthy of their ideals.

Howard Thurman, in his *Meditations of the Heart*, advanced the same principle. He asked: "Are you a reservoir, or are you a canal or a swamp?"[37] Leadership surfacing from a liberating spirituality must come from a reservoir. It must be an example of the greatest sense of integrity.

Finally, we must "talk the talk and walk the walk." Our society suggests that the worth of persons has more to do with image, material objects, and other symbols of status than it does the character and contributions of individuals. Our market-driven, consumer-oriented society perpetuates the myth that what we have is who we are. Materialism has infected our society and our individual lives. The name on the clothes or shoes is more important, it would appear, than the item itself.

Liberating leadership is of a nature that it teaches and preaches that the ultimate worth of a person begins and ends with God. What we wear, what we drive, the house we inhabit are not true symbols of our worth. Our worth is grounded in a hidden wholeness, revealed by God. Our worth, as people of God, is beyond comparison. We are a "chosen race, a royal priesthood, a holy nation, God's own people" (1 Pet. 2:9). Persons displaying liberating spiritual leadership will also live their lives congruent with this fundamental truth.

Jesus usually redirected the attention of his followers away from himself and toward the Creator. Men and women who attempt to be servants and attentive listeners, who lead honest and liberated lives, will foster communities and individuals awakened to the hidden wholeness. This is happening today as persons are providing leadership driven by a liberating spirituality.

Liberating Leadership in the African American Community

In chapter 3 we highlighted four congregations and their pastors who, for us, illustrated the kind of ministry settings and clergy leadership we advocate in this book. The Reverend Dr. Cynthia Hale of Decatur, Georgia; the Reverend Dr. Jeremiah Wright of Chicago, Illinois; the Reverend Dr. Carl Brown of Marks, Mississippi; and the Reverend Dr. Cecil Williams of San Francisco, California, were discussed in some detail. As we reflect on additional contemporary leadership, in both clergy and laity, other names come to mind. African American women and men who display a kind of community leadership that appears to be grounded in a liberating spirituality are plentiful. We will highlight only a few among the many who exist. Our reason for mentioning the names of these persons is not to suggest that they are perfect in all ways. They may not model a liberating spirituality in terms of leadership styles, in one overall uniform fashion; but as we seek leadership that is needed in our own churches and local communities, these are the kinds of people we may offer as examples of effective, empowered, and empowering leaders.

Retired bishop Leontyne C. Kelly of the United Methodist church and Bishop Barbara Harris of the Episcopal church are key persons among clergywomen. Rev. Dr. Barbara King of the Hillside International Truth Center in Atlanta, Georgia, and Rev. Johnnie Coleman of the Christ Universal Temple in Chicago are charismatic preachers and leaders among large congregations.

African Methodist Episcopal bishops John Hurst Adams and John R. Bryant are two examples of persons who have provided liberating leadership in and beyond their denominations. The former pastor of Brooklyn's Concord Baptist Church, Rev. Gardner C. Taylor; Rev. (Congressman) Floyd Flake of Allen African Methodist Episcopal Church in Queens, New York; Rev. Johnny Ray Youngblood at St. Paul Community Baptist Church, Brooklyn, New York; and Rev. Jonathan Greer, pastor of the Cathedral of Faith Church of God in Christ, Atlanta, Georgia, are persons who, in so many creative ways, have provided liberating leadership in their communities and beyond. Other pastors could and should be mentioned, but the point is that there are persons, active in their churches and cities, who are enthusiastically working with God's people. They are active in African American communities, churches, schools, and families. They have been called by God to lead other men and women to an awareness of God's liberating encounter, liberating reflection, and liberating action. They have been empowered spiritually and have chosen to participate with God in God's empowering activity in the world.

There are lay women and men who have modeled for their communities this kind of liberating spirituality. Fred Williams, a community activist in the Los Angeles area, is an example. In response to a series of drive-by shootings being directed at Latino families in that city, Mr. Williams decided to act. He encouraged other African American young people to join him and sleep in the homes of certain Hispanic families. It is reported that "a clear message was sent and the violence subsided."[38] This man helped to liberate a community. Individuals, when empowered spiritually from within and without, can help to transform communities.

Empowering Parents: Mamie's Tale

As Mamie tried to sleep at night, she was kept awake by some particular and recurring concerns in her community. One seemed to present itself with a gnawing insistence. There was an unusually high incidence of teen pregnancy and teenaged mothers among African Americans in her community. Something had to be done. It was a burden on her mind and on her heart.

Mamie had participated in the training program and subsequent activities of a project on "Developing Leaders, Building Communities," sponsored by ITC. So she wrote to the project director, expressing her concern and articulating a need and a passion to respond: "At this time in my community, there is a whole lot of brokenness and unwholesomeness going on. My children in my community are suffering the most. And my heart is continuously open to their pains. . . . I am strongly motivated to change the situation here."[39]

Empowering Parents for Troubled Times, Inc., came into being as a result of a vision that Mamie and others held of responding to an identified and perceived need in their Greene County, Georgia, community. This vision arose out of participation in the ITC project referenced above. The project was designed to help rural citizens increase their involvement in identifying and solving problems in their communities.

Over the last three years, with some help from ITC and other institutions, including the University of Georgia, Mamie Hillman has labored with partners and begun to make a difference. Empowering Parents for Troubled Times, Inc., has obtained their 501(c) 3 status. (Under this code, a public nonprofit corporation that is exempt from taxation may be established.) A doctoral candidate in social work from the University of Georgia is one among a cadre of volunteers. Mamie had taken seriously the concept that educational institutions exist to serve the communities in which they are set. This organization is aggressively pursuing and receiving funding to support their work.

A recent activity illustrates the widespread influence and effect of the work of Mamie Hillman and Empowering Parents for Troubled Times, Inc. With other community agencies as partners, they sponsored a teen pregnancy and parenting symposium, entitled "'It Takes a Village': Our Sons and Daughters as Parents." This particular event was preceded by organizing efforts which brought together churches, pastors, and people across denominational and racial lines.

The vision that energized the work which resulted in the symposium is expressed in a statement in the symposium brochure:

> Let us look at our children and families in our community, not as blurred objects in the landscape, or by their possible usefulness to us; but to see them with a consecrated focus (imagination), with the "eyes of the heart" with faith in their possibilities. . . . It is a great loss when we look at children/families from a financial or business point of view and neglect the life side (spiritual).[40]

This statement interprets the theme of the symposium and reminds us of the nature of life in community. It affects all persons in the totality of their beings. It expresses a sense of the spirituality of which we are writing and further supports the perspective of our common bond as human beings. In good times and in difficult times, we are together. An African proverb puts it: "Rain falls on all the village huts."

These and the many others we could have listed are persons who continue to show us how to get together and not pull away. They have chosen a style of leadership that, we argue, is grounded in the hidden wholeness of our God. They themselves, along with those persons who work assertively with them, have discovered the God of all creation. Ours is a God who seeks to bring us together "in an inescapable network of mutuality."[41] This is the way we were made. This is what God intended. We invite you to claim with us this existential reality and affirm that God calls us into community. It is this fundamental principle of a spirituality of hidden wholeness that we will explore in our final chapter.

In this chapter, we have explored our common and interconnected life. We are not alone, confronting our society and world by ourselves; we are in this together. And together, in the community, active in the church, growing within the school, and nurtured in the family, the African American individual and collectivity has claimed this shared reality. They and we have discovered and continue to ascertain a liberating spirituality which leads us all toward greater wholeness. It is true that we are all clothed "in a single garment of destiny."

After you consider the following questions for reflection and action, we encourage you to join God's journey toward an interconnected community (chapter 5).

Questions for Reflection and Action

1. An African proverb states: "I am because we are. We are because I am." How do you find this to be true for you and for your life with others? Illustrate also from what you know of this lifestyle in Africa and among Africans in the diaspora. In what ways does such a worldview express an affirmation that can be made by persons who believe in one God?

2. What are some understandings you have of "community" in the immediate situation and in the human family in the world? How do these perspectives affect the way you relate to and treat other persons?

3. Read again 1 Corinthians 12. In what ways does this scripture express our interrelatedness in the human family? Does it provide a realistic basis for helping persons make such a common affirmation? List reasons in support of or in opposition to your perspective.

4. What were some of the strengths of your (extended) family as you were growing up? How can we build on those strengths in family formation and maintenance? How can the church accentuate some of those gifts—past and present—of family?

5. What were some of the ways you encountered the hidden wholeness of God in your family, school, and church in the past? How can
we help others experience that today—in family life, school activities, and as a part of the church?

5

"He's Got the Whole World in His Hands"

Our Future Calling

He's got the whole world in His hands,
He's got the big round world in His hands,
He's got the whole world in His hands,
He's got the whole world in His hands.[1]

Throughout this text we have advocated the liberating aspects of spirituality, its encounter, reflection, and action. We believe that God is the one who initiates this liberation from within the center of our being (the individual) and in the midst of our everyday activity (the collective) in the world. God creates us as persons in community in such a way that we can experience ourselves, others, and God in a liberating and open-ended fashion. As incredible as it might appear, African and African American men and women have held to this God in the midst of overwhelming suffering and pain. They have in the past and continue to forge a spirituality that could only be described as liberating. This spirituality has enabled many people of color to both claim their sorrow and express their joy. This is the story we have attempted to tell in this book.

It is a story that began years prior to the invasion of Africa and the subsequent slave trade. The spirituality of the various African peoples is at the center of our story. The spirituals were early affirmations of faith for the slave ancestors of today's African American people. They express what the slaves' faith affirmations about God were for them. Affirmations of faith have their foundation in God's self-disclosure about God's personhood and God's relationship to

God's people. Thus, the spirituals offer us clues of how the slave ancestors of African Americans experienced, understood, and claimed
God for themselves, even in the midst of the dehumanizing condition that was slavery.

The song "He's Got the Whole World in His Hands" is an affirmation of faith in the tradition and heritage of African American
spirituality. It expresses not only that God is Creator of the universe,
but that God is in control of the whole world that has been created.
The whole world includes not only nature but persons: you and me,
brother, sister, and even the "little bitty baby."

Cheryl Kirk-Duggan has suggested in a womanist reading that
this "God is a personal, powerful, compassionate, liberating God
who encompasses masculine and feminine qualities and cares about
an individual's circumstances."[2] As they sang "Sometimes I Feel
Like a Motherless Child," slave ancestors also affirmed the knowledge that "trouble don't last always." We might add from the
African and African American perspective that such an understanding was always inclusive and communal.

"He's Got the Whole World in His Hands" is an affirmation of
faith, not only that God is in control of the world, but that God will
override all the evil intentions of human beings to acknowledge our
oneness in God. Our future calling, as our present calling, is to recognize those situations where this affirmation of God's sovereignty
is manifest. As we work constantly for its ongoing recognition, the
hidden wholeness will be revealed.

Unfortunately many of us don't live our lives as if the hidden
wholeness existed or were readily accessible. The destructive ways
we find to treat each other in terms of economic distribution, race,
and gender simply point to this social reality. We appear to live in
a world that too often displays economic injustice, racism, and
sexism, and less often a kind of core spirituality that could begin
to liberate us from these evils. Our world has become disenchanted—slowly but surely losing its mysterious, spiritually liberating foundation. There is a wholeness about creation, but it remains
hidden in many ways because we choose individual disobedience
and collective blindness rather than what God intended. The Divine
intention was that we experience God's totality, even in the midst of
suffering and oppression. The African American church has found

a way to make that happen—to celebrate God who created humankind for wholeness and empowers human beings' liberating encounters, reflection, and action—when that wholeness appears to be lacking. The black church, in its finest hour, has modeled a transformative kind of liberation that points us in a needed direction. We need God to confront the principalities and powers of this world that encourage individual and collective annihilation. We must celebrate with God as God empowers us to discover joy in the wholeness of God's community.

This discovery enables us to reconnect with God's creation—both the earth and its people. It helps us affirm that we are not alone, we are part of one great whole. The African American community and its essential institutions (church, school, and family) have historically maintained this fundamental truth. We are in this together. We can neither survive nor progress unless we do so together. This is a message many in American society have simply ignored. Our American forms of individualism, competition, and bottom-line rationalization have undercut this possibility. As a result, we all participate in the diminution of our society, but worse still, the slow disappearance of God's intended wholeness. Again, we argue that the African American context, when it has intentionally celebrated its core values of community and interrelatedness, has fought this American seduction. This especially has occurred in the black church and spilled over into the school and family. African American community leadership has been just that, when these values have not only been encouraged but demanded. In reality, this is the calling of all leadership. This is God's calling to us.

As we have indicated throughout this book, God is the ground of our being and the source of our interconnected community. God has created us to be whole, and experience one another in wholeness. God is actively pursuing us to join God in the discovery of God's hidden wholeness.

God's Activity in the World

Fundamental to our theological enterprise is the belief that in God's "hand is the life of every living thing and the breath of every human being" (Job 12:10). We do claim, in our better moments, that God does have the whole world in God's hands. While there is significant evidence that would challenge that faith stance, we operate within a Christian tradition that professes that credo. God is ultimately in control of existence as we have come to discover it. Complex evil forces—both individual and systemic—are raging in our presence, yet God is encouraging all of creation to move toward God's own desired end. This understanding is not unique to Christian tradition and theology. Traditional African religions and many other religions of the world have, in various ways, laid claim to this affirmation about that "One" we call God.

An Akan proverb says, "God is like a baobab tree, no one human being can embrace God." The baobab tree is a familiar sight in West Africa. It has an extremely huge trunk. It is so expansive that no one human being can wrap his/her arms around it. The proverb is appropriate for talking about God. No one people, tribe, nation, or religion can claim God exclusively.

"Religion in Africa, like all religions, is a profound apprehension of a truth which is not of [human] making, a truth whose significance originates from the fact that its validity does not depend on the [human] mind."[3] It is therefore presumptuous of one people to claim that it has the understanding of God to which other peoples of the world must subscribe. Another African proverb offers a proper perspective in this matter: "It is through other people's wisdom that we learn wisdom ourselves; a single person's understanding does not amount to anything."[4]

God has revealed God's self to the different peoples of the world in a plethora of forms. It would seem to be rather naive to assume otherwise. We most certainly affirm this understanding. God is God and no one of us can authoritatively suggest that he or she, as a finite being, has the absolute final word on God's self-revelation. God does what God chooses; we are only recipients of God's disclosure.

However, our personal experience has been one that flows from the Christian perspective. All three of us grew up in different cultural settings. Our backgrounds include an African American experience, an Afro-Caribbean heritage, and a European American perspective, as we shared in the introduction. Our personal journeys have not been the same, but our desired destinations appear to be complementary. All three of us are Christian ministers teaching in a Protestant theological seminary. We responded to the call of God in Jesus Christ and seek to be obedient to God within that vocation. While our life experiences have at times been significantly different, we claim one another as Christian brothers. We affirm our kinship in the body of Christ. This is our common religious tradition.

We, like others in the Christian community, celebrate the trinitarian understandings about God. Recognizing God as Creator, Redeemer, and Sustainer of our faith is important to our perspective. Traditionally, the language of the Christian church has incorporated the notion of God as Father, Son, and Holy Spirit. In the third chapter, we recounted the traditional language of the African Methodist Episcopal church in its affirmation of the "Fatherhood of God and the brotherhood of men." This basic, yet essential biblical doctrine of the "parenthood of God and the kinship of all peoples," is vital to our experience of God in our society and world.

God created us. God is the author of life and community. God is the ground of our being, the source of existence as we know it.

The Word became flesh in the person of Jesus of Nazareth. His birth, life, death, and resurrection offer us the incarnate and redeeming presence of the Holy One. We discover the glory of God in the life and ministry of Jesus. We rediscover God's creative purpose for humankind in this man, Jesus. The way he related to others models for us that intended relationship God desires. The love of God and the love of others as oneself were first authentically seen in the one we call Redeemer.

Finally, God does not leave us alone. God is present with us in both our private lives and communal experiences. God is friend, advocate, Divine presence. We find the strength we need, in community and in individual acts of courage, through the perpetual remembrance of the truth of Christ—through the power of the Holy Spirit.

"It Don't Mean a Thing If It Ain't Got That Swing": James's Tale and All That Jazz

Preaching had been in James's family for three previous generations. He wasn't about to make it a fourth. Yet he lived under a sense of

God's presence, in the fulfillment of a promise that James claims has been real in so many experiences on his life's journey. It is: "Lo! I am with you always."

One Christmas he got a saxophone for a present from a father he never really knew. Actually, James confesses that that was the only interaction that he has had with his father. Having lived mostly without a father, his dependence is on God, who promised "Lo! I am with you always." Yet the knowledge of the promise being fulfilled is always in hindsight. If we are to discern God's presence, we must be aware of how unmerited God's favor can be. It is often when we are surprised by God's goodness that we more readily discern God's presence.

This is what James learned in the mountains of Europe where he had gone, with friends, playing the saxophone. For it in those mountains, far away from home, he was almost killed. "Lo! I am with you always." James went to Europe on the understanding that God "has a chance for you." That chance came at his mother's sacrifice. So James prayed at that point of crisis, in a country far away from home, "Don't let me get killed, let me survive." Survive for what? "If I am going to preach, let me preach later. I am a musician." But James was not the only person praying. As he expresses it, he "was prayed up." Many persons, including his mother, were praying for him. God's presence is in the community of those who call God's name. Those who pray enable God's sustaining presence to be known even by those who establish barriers and boundaries against God in their lives.

The soul recognizes that God's presence has been in the varying situations of life. It also discovers the claim that God makes on lives and acknowledges "God's hand is on me." The point of yielding is reached with the testimony, "I preach to live and live to preach." And the saxophone and "all that jazz," with all those swings, become part of the ministry and the awareness of God's presence.

Invitation to Journey: To Follow Where God Is Leading

This creating, redeeming, and sustaining God beckons all of us to join others in the journey toward wholeness and community.

Shalom or "wholeness" is the intended goal for the human family, not division and separation. We are called to be in community with one another equally participating in the discovery of our common objective. Ours is a God of justice and peace, judgment and reconciliation, brokenness and completeness. God invites us to participate with God in the recreation of our world and society, always moving in the direction of God's will and plan for our lives. We do so in profound humility because we know that God goes before us, God is with us, and God covers our rear! Many times it takes painful experiences to remind us of that reality. But thank God we have remembered.

We are disciples of the One who goes before us. We are followers in the truest sense of the word. We have been called by God to participate in authentic and bold ways in the world—according to God's leading. Those of us who have a leadership role in the church, both laity and clergy, always point beyond ourselves to the One who maps the way. We choose to lead because we have been led. We hope we have arrived on the battlefield with some word from God! Otherwise, our efforts are most often counterproductive.

The challenge is discerning where God is leading us. There are multiple historical examples of persons and groups who thought they were discerning correctly the will of God and discovered something quite different. The Jonestown community of Guyana and the experience among David Koresh's followers in Waco, Texas, are but two fairly recent occurrences. It is not always simple to discern the will of God.

Perceiving God's will and having the courage to be obedient to it are also challenges. The "courage to be" (Tillich) in the world as a follower of Christ Jesus, in a genuine and daring fashion, is called for in our society—yet often unheeded.

This is why the local congregation, the community of faith, is so vital. It is within community, among our brothers and sisters who have responded positively to the call of Christ, that we can aspire to discern God's activity. We can realize an individual and collective courage needed to be obedient in the face of overwhelming odds. We can dare to be courageous. We can choose to be obedient.

As we worship, create a learning environment, provide congregational care, reach out to the community and beyond, and do advocacy for the least among us, it is in the church that we can remind ourselves of God's vision for the human family. We can tell our story, hear the story of others, and participate in the making of a new story. We can see our individual and congregational story within the framework of the larger Christian story. Rehearsing the Christian story and seeing its intersection with our own—both private and collective—is one of the primary ways in which we begin to discern the activity of God. It is not coincidental that Christ Jesus said that we see God in the stranger, the one experiencing hunger, the men or women confined in prisons. God can be found in the lives and experiences of those who appear to be forgotten, lost, or on the margins of society. The Christian story seems to reveal this over and over again.

Our discernment of God's will and activity in the world is blocked at those points in our congregational life where we are blind to those principalities and powers that work against it. Economic injustice is not a part of the Christian story; distribution of wealth and resources is. Racism is not intended in God's revelation in Christ Jesus; the body of Christ is. Sexism is a result of collective and individual blindness, not the way the Christian story unfolds in the lives of God's men and women, boys and girls. Anyone or anything that posits a hierarchical ordering of existence—rich over poor, white over black, male over female—is not true to the Christian story. Any institution, denomination, or other entity that would argue for the stratification of persons or groups of persons based on class, race, or gender is working against our God and God's purposes. When that occurs, the disobedience of God's people is more in evidence than God's intended goal for humanity.

This disobedience is lessened when we gather as a community of faith around a central task. That task, we argue, is one of discovery. *All* of us, even in our diversity of gifts, cultures, and experiences, must come together seeking the one thing most needed. At the core of our being, all of us are hungry. We long for completeness as individual selves and as members of a larger whole. We are groping for what we, the authors of this text, call the hidden wholeness. We are looking for the One who created us, redeems us, and sustains us in all of our living. A liberating encounter with God, reflection on that encounter, and action that flows from that encounter/reflection form the basis of a kind of authentic spirituality needed in our society and in our lives. The African American experience of intense suffering and empowering joy provided the crucible for discovering that liberating spirituality. The whole of the Christian community longs for this self-discovery. It is past time to reveal that the hidden wholeness of our existence is readily available. God can help us if we choose to help ourselves.

Prerequisites for God's help are repentance and conversion. These are topics we will address in the next section. Coupled with that, the broader Christian community needs to learn to work together. We must reach across the community and communities in the Christian enterprise. Shared leadership, empowered through a mutually liberating spirituality, could enable us to share our stories and see our commonality within the greater Christian story. Building coalitions, building on a participatory mutuality is greatly needed in the Christian world. Once realized, it can move us toward a more fully developed participation with God—in God's way, in God's world.

Working Hand in Hand: Transforming Sandy Bottom to Sandy Vista

In Ensley, just outside of Birmingham, a community was in decay. Abandoned buildings and empty lots were filled with trash: beer bottles and cans, some half-empty. But people still lived there. Down Avenue D, small green shack homes present a uniform view. These buildings were part of the housing built between 1920 and 1940 for employees of the old U.S. Steel Ensley Steelworks. Then when the Ensley Works closed in 1984, the attendant social ills became evident. Unemployment, out-migration and its consequent decrease in population, rise in the crime rate, increase in drug traffic, all became markedly noticeable.

Into such a situation Ron Nored[5] entered as a student appointment from his bishop. There he met Deacon Clarence Brown. One day, amidst the blight and decay, they caught a vision of a transformed community. They began talking about it, and others began to see what they could see. And thus BEAT was born. (BEAT is an acronym for Bethel [the AME church of which Nored is pastor] Ensley [the community] Action Task, Inc.) Nored has continued in the appointment beyond his graduation from Interdenominational Theological Center in 1989.

BEAT has been able to bring together churches and their leaders from the metropolitan Birmingham area, architects, volunteer laborers, unskilled and skilled, in a community-revitalization project. Its objective: the rebuilding of Ensley's Sandy Bottom neighborhood. BEAT has met together regularly over the last five years to establish goals and pursue strategies, empower people to work to realize the vision of a transformed neighborhood.

It all started with a vision that Ron Nored and Clarence Brown shared with church members and other persons in the community— both challenging and inviting them to share the vision, explore the possibilities, identify the resources, and make the commitment to transformation.

Blacks and whites, adults and children, young and old started by clearing the trash away in a six-block area between Avenue C and Avenue E and 14th and 17th streets. They picked up those empty beer bottles and worn-out car tires. They hacked away at mounds of dead, tangled grass. All that was five years ago.

Today, the project is almost complete as families have been able to move into affordable housing. None of the current residents, a significant number of whom were elderly, was displaced. Nored's idea of building more than houses—building homes and building a community—has caught on. Persons take pride in their homes. They have worked together on one another's units. They have planted trees and cultivated flower gardens. They have formed a neighborhood association which meets regularly to talk about what they, as residents, need to have and do to make it hospitable and safe for all who live and visit there. They have a new self-concept as a community. Sandy Bottom is now Sandy Vista.

Discovery of the Hidden Wholeness

We live in a diverse, multicultural society. It is not a melting pot, as some would assume. Nor should it be. We have our own particularities, in terms of gender, ethnicity, race, and religion. Our particularities are especially noteworthy when we affirm our cultural differences. Many of us see the world and one another through different cultural lenses. That is a wonderful reality that we should embrace here in the United States. We are fortunate to have many different peoples, from most parts of the world, as a part of our American scene. We are richly blessed with the expansive and unique gifts and graces of different persons. When we see ourselves as we ought, both in terms of our particularities and commonalities, we are like a mosaic—"a piece of inlaid work composed of bits of stone or glass which form a pattern or a picture."[6] We must come to a point in our history and life together where we celebrate, with enthusiasm, the peculiar and particular cultural gifts each of us offers North American society.

Even those of us who call ourselves Christians differ significantly in our appropriation and interpretation of the faith. The terms "conservative" and "liberal," "religious right" and "left," are bandied about in our various forms of media. When we introduce the term "spirituality" we recognize that there are a variety of Christian spiritualities. Diversity exists there also.

As we draw on the diverse elements of our biblical record, our differences surface. Different traditions of the Christian faith developed, in some ways, by their correspondence to different spiritualities.

> There is, for instance, in the Old Testament, the peculiar spirituality of the pilgrim people of the exodus tradition, that of royal tradition of the two kingdoms of Israel and Judah, priestly tradition in Jerusalem, the wisdom spirituality of the sages, that of the "anawin" (God's poor ones), and that of the apocalyptic visionaries. All of these various biblical spiritualities have been challenged by the prophets and reinterpreted for new times and circumstances. All such tradition and their corresponding spiritualities were taken up and radically reinterpreted in the New Testament in the light of the life, death, and resurrection of Jesus.[7]

The wealth of the plurality of spiritualities that exist suggests that we have many resources and insights to draw upon in our Christian journey—across ecumenical and cross-cultural lines. This should be encouraged and not ignored. The ways we read the Bible and interpret Christian discipleship are shaped by the cultures and multiple experiences that have formed us. We too quickly can make our own cultural lenses an absolute or succumb to the fruit of idolatry when we close our minds and hearts against the diversity of our population. We are many people shaped by various manifestations of ethnicity, race, and Christian interpretation. As we hear and value our different voices, male and female, African American, European American, Asian American, Hispanic, American Indian, and others, we are a stronger human community.

Yet within the legitimate diversity of our cultures and their various spiritualities, there are some basic features which we affirm as being common to Christian experience. There are some marks of Christian spirituality that appear to us to be fairly consistent. We are not reaching for a universal substance because we celebrate our mosaic combination of variety. But we argue that one fundamental experience appears to be common in the human endeavor. All of us, it would seem, long for something more. We hunger. We thirst. We are looking and longing for something beyond our grasp. It is as Augustine, that great North African bishop of the early church, said: We hunger for God. "Thou awakest us to delight in praising thee; for thou hast made us for thyself and our hearts are restless till they find rest in thee."[8]

The way this works itself out in the Christian community is through the person of Jesus. Our Christian spirituality centers on following Christ. His birth, life, death, and resurrection are of particular importance to those of us who seek to be his followers. The events of the cross and resurrection provide a core set of realities about God and God's intention for humankind. God gave us one Savior to follow. Christian spirituality involves following that one, to live in God's presence, with the totality of our being and action, in the midst of the sufferings and struggles of the good earth.

We hunger and thirst. We long for completeness—as individuals and as communities. That thirst can be quenched, according to our Christian tradition, in the incarnate One, Christ Jesus our Savior. God gave the Divine Self in the person of Jesus. Those of us who decide to be disciples can begin to taste "living water." We can discover that the wholeness of God has been in our midst all along. We can participate in the unveiling of the hidden wholeness.

This happens in various ways. It is experienced and interpreted in a plurality of forms. But the process, we argue, remains the same. As we seek God, we encounter God. As we encounter God, we reflect on that encounter. As we reflect on that encounter, we decide to act. As we act, we encounter God. And the process repeats itself. In fact, we often participate in the world, offering ourselves and our resources to be used by God for God's people, and discover that God is already there. Encounter, reflection, and action; *or* action, reflection, encounter: This is a liberating process that is cyclical and not progressive.

The Christian story reveals its central character as being from Nazareth. We encounter the man Jesus in the temple when he clearly articulated his mission and thus revealed to us, his disciples, our contemporary task: "The Spirit of [God] is upon me, because [God] has anointed me to bring good news to the poor. [God] has sent me to proclaim release to the captives and recovery of sight to the blind, to let the oppressed go free, to proclaim the year of [God]'s favor" (Luke 4:18–19).

To Proclaim Liberation: A Vision and a Task

The expression "to proclaim liberty" occurs in the Old Testament in a specific context, that of the Jubilee Year. The priestly document, Leviticus, gives very detailed legislation on how to celebrate the Jubilee Year. Every fiftieth year is to be declared sacred. "And you shall hallow the fiftieth year and you shall proclaim liberty throughout the land to all its inhabitants" (Lev. 25:10).

The expression *"qara'derór"* ("proclaim liberty") which is also found in Isaiah 61:1 comes from Leviticus 25:10. The word *"derór"* is not frequently used in the Old Testament. The translation in the Greek Old Testament is not *eleutheria* (freedom). The usual translation is *aphesis,* which really means "letting go, release." It also means "forgiveness, acquittal."

These ideas of Jubilee Year inform the declaration of Jesus at Nazareth. Jesus recalls the elements and the dimensions of the Jubilee Year. They are a challenge and a call to those who seek to discover this hidden wholeness. They have to do with economic relations, attitudes to work and property, and most of all with human relations. They all point to a common life wherein the affirmations of our interrelatedness are made. These arrangements, in our life together as human beings, are possible as we become liberated. We set ourselves free from those things to which we cling and commit ourselves to God who reveals to us, with eyes that God gives, what God is making possible.

Along with his announcement of the coming of the dominion or reign of God and the many parables that depicted what the coming might look like, Jesus, the anointed teacher among us, illustrated what we are to do. What we are to do (action) if we desire to discover (encounter/reflection) the essence of our heart's desire is to follow him into the world. It is there that we find God, God's people, and God's human community. It is there that we reunite with the other members of the body of Christ. It is there that we begin to see that wholeness that previously escaped our vision.

This is a challenge for us, because outside our doors there are men and women, girls and boys who are suffering. Similar to those described in the Lukan text, there are those who are captives, many who are poor, others both blind and oppressed. Jesus' mission is our mission at present; it is a mission of liberation. The proclamation of "the year of [God]'s favor" is long overdue. The story must be rehearsed, shared and modeled for the masses. It must help us unveil the hidden wholeness of God.

As followers of Christ, we see ourselves and others as members of the one body. We celebrate our variety of gifts and services. We offer different activities. But "to each is given the manifestation of the Spirit for the common good," says Paul in writing to the church at Corinth (1 Cor. 12:7). In fact, it is "the same God who activates all of them in everyone" (1 Cor. 12:6)—gifts, services, and activities. We are many members, but significant parts of one overall body of Christ. "For just as the body is one and has many members, and all the members of the body, though many, are one body, so it is with Christ. For in the one Spirit we were all baptized into one body— Jews or Greeks, slaves or free—and we were all made to drink of one Spirit" (1 Cor. 12:12–13).

We thirst for the "drink of one Spirit" that will satisfy. We hunger for the one that can give us completeness. And though we bring our various particularities to the gathering we call the body of Christ, we have one God, one Jesus, and one Spirit. We are in this together, one human family, under one head. And our responsibility to one another, even with our variety of gifts and services, is awesome. Paul reminds us that the members of the body of Christ are interconnected and interrelated. "If one member suffers, all suffer together with it; if one member is honored, all rejoice together with it" (1 Cor. 12:26). Dr. King added to this when he said:

> As long as there is poverty in this world, no [one] can be totally rich even if he [or she] has a billion dollars. As long as diseases are rampant and millions of people cannot expect to live more than twenty or thirty years, no [one] can be totally healthy, even if [she or] he just got a clean bill of health from the finest clinic in America. Strangely enough, I can never be what I ought to be until you are what you ought to be. You can never be what you ought to be until I am what I ought to be. This is the way the world is made.[9]

This is the way God created the world. God intended for the human family to live in community as interrelated members. Jesus came into the world to call us back to that body or community. But we have been disobedient and disloyal to this greater vision.

We have allowed ourselves to be blinded to the wholeness of God's creation. We have chosen to avoid or ignore the transforming purpose of God and God's people. We have not always allowed ourselves to participate with God in God's propelling presence in acts of justice, righteousness, and peace. We have been inattentive to the social problems of economic injustice, racism, and sexism and their underlying evil of a "world disenchanted." We have not always been courageous or willing to follow obediently the One who goes before us—the One who reveals the hidden wholeness.

We have sinned against God and our brothers and sisters. We have served ourselves and not others. We have undercut the possibility of building up the body or creating community. We need to be forgiven if we are to go on from here.

Repentance precedes forgiveness. Conversion follows repentance. And reparation flows from conversion. These are the essentials that we, who are called to leadership in the Christian community, must claim for ourselves and others on the journey toward wholeness. There is no other way. We cannot discover or rediscover the hidden wholeness of God until we shed our blindness or blinding ways.

The scriptures of the Old and New Testament emphasize our need for repentance. The leaders of Israel recognized the necessity of repentance based on self-examination. Solomon stood before the assembly of Israel and prayed that his people would "come to their senses in the land of their captors, saying, 'We have sinned, and have done wrong; we have acted wickedly'" (1 Kings 8:47). David, even with his immense powers, was crushed by the awareness of his sin against God and his people. He was humbled and brought to utter remorse as he looked at himself. John the Baptist and Jesus called the people to repentance. They articulated that conversion or transformation would not be possible unless the people saw their acts of separation from God and one another, and turned back to God. Paul invited his hearers to shed their sinful nature and become new persons. He called them into a life of radical change and new self-understanding.

The key here is the movement away from blindness of one's sin and toward an awareness of it. Repentance is not possible for the individual who continues to be blind to her or his individualized self-interest in the face of great social needs and problems. Transformation, beginning with personal repentance, is not going to happen when persons refuse to see their individual and collective participation in social sin. Repentance means seeing one's sinful acts and participation in evil social systems as they really are. David had to confess "I am the one" who sinned against God. So must we.

In the face of our social sinfulness, individual repentance is required. We are to acknowledge our acts of cooperation that foster the economic exploitation of others. We must see the ways in which we choose to participate in sexist and racist institutional acts. We must claim our personal participation in these social sins of our society and world. But that is not sufficient. Individual confession and personal conversion will not eradicate problems of systemic evil. Individual change is needed. But in addition to personal acts of transformation, social reparation is necessary. Society, as a whole, requires alteration. Trends and patterns that oppress individuals and whole groups of people will need to be reversed. Acts of reparation will be required for a more comprehensive transformation.

The conversion or transformation of an individual often brings acts of reparation. When Zacchaeus experienced transformation in his encounter with Jesus, he determined that acts of reparation were required. He responded to the forgiving love of Jesus by saying, "Look, half of my possessions . . . I will give to the poor; and if I have defrauded anyone of anything, I will pay back four times as much" (Luke 19:8). Zacchaeus recognized that his personal repentance and restoration were not sufficient. He acknowledged that his exploitation of the poor through fraudulent taxation required making amends. He could not simply be sorry for his sin, he must pay reparation. He must attempt to rectify his past actions with actual repayment of extorted funds. Repentance leads to reparation in Zacchaeus' conversion experience.

The movement from individual repentance to a collective spirit of social reparation is critical for those of us who seek God's hidden wholeness and desire to lead others toward it. We must provide a kind of leadership among the body of Christ that models this movement. A true encounter with God must always force us to reflect on our unworthiness and utter inadequacy. The most appropriate action following that encounter/reflection is usually one of confession, repentance, and reparation.

This has remained a fairly consistent pattern in the Christian story throughout the centuries. God calls us back to God's intended vision of humankind. We repent of our participation in those individual and collective acts that work against that vision. We join others in communal acts of reparation, working with God as God restores God's creation. What was hidden becomes visible again!

Recognizing and Affirming an Interconnected Community

As we discover our hidden wholeness we begin to see the interconnectedness of world, society, and all people. Our spirituality drives us both within and without. We discern our inner hunger and recognize that same reality among the variety of brothers and sisters beyond our personal vision. We find that we are all in this together. An awareness of a potentially interconnected community becomes a motivating force in our individual and communal life.

Spirituality that emerged from the African and African American experience has affirmed this interconnected community all along. In community, we experience rejection, bruising, brokenness. We stumble, we fall. But it is also in community that we know welcome, we experience a sense of belonging. We find sanctuary, healing, and wholeness.

In our community—the place where we work and where we sense and experience kinship—life's experiences of disease and suffering, loss and death seem to have been more pronounced of late. Maybe it is because our immediate community is small. It is at these points of life's experiences that the nature and the quality of life together become patently manifest. In a real sense, community cannot be created by us. Yet it is our responsibility to express through our lives— in word and deed, through our lifestyles—ways in which our common life is informed by God's presence. It is God in our midst who gives us eyes to see the hidden wholeness.

Reflection on Life and Death in a Community

Approximately three hours after Lillian died, Tom joined us—his community—in our refectory. The school had just completed its reaccreditation review visit. The evaluation team had done their work and gone. Some of us were meeting in several small clusters. Tom came and joined one group. We had received word of her death earlier. Someone inquired if he wished something to eat. He did, and another got him a plate. One by one, others of us gathered around expressing our sharing. A word here. A hug, an embrace there. Some shared words, as led by the Spirit. Then we joined hands and prayed. The prayer ended, and after a pause and a brief greeting—an assurance of solidarity in sorrow—we slipped away. Carolyn, a close colleague on the faculty, lingered and kept him company. Community is manifest in our finding one another through mutual trust. In the African American experience and grounded in our African roots, this relationship is expressed in the words, "I am because we are.

We are because I am." As individuals, we are not persons, we find our personhood in community.

Death instructs us, informs us about life and immortality. Lillian's death taught Tom most penetratingly and meaningfully about the concept of death and immortality. As he expressed it, he never conceived of immortality as a realistic or viable concept before.

> The verse of scripture that helped (me) had to do with the fact that "from dust thou art and to dust returneth." The concept of Mother Earth opened tremendous vistas for me when I looked at it. I like to play around in the yard and garden with roses, that sort of thing. It's always fascinating to me that I feed them all the same fertilizer, give them all the same work and I pull the weeds. And this bush will produce a red rose and the one $2\frac{1}{2}$ feet away from it will produce a pink one, and the commonality of this is the Earth.
>
> But I had to go to the cemetery to see what, how is this possible. I talked with the keeper and he told me that though we require that you put the coffin in a vault, the vault has a life span, it doesn't last forever. And eventually it will disintegrate and indeed the anatomy within the coffin does unite with the Earth which is the Mother of all living, either directly or indirectly. So that all these precious metals, the diamonds, all of this is plucked out of the Earth.
>
> I looked at my neighbor's lawn before he had cut it the first time and I could see all these, literally hundreds, little oaks growing up, which indicates how many of the acorns became fertile. I knew that they would not have a chance because they would get cut with the lawn. But then as an example of the possibility of that, there is this giant oak that is so large that I can't get my arms around the trunk, started from this little thing and makes the whole concept of immortality much more interesting.
>
> The other thing that jumped out at me from this had to do with generosity. It doesn't make any difference who you are, what your portfolio is, that you give it up at this event, and if you have some real concerns about that, you will decide before the event actually takes place how you want this to be handled so you do what we call making a will. But you make it with the intent that somebody else will. It will be somebody else's responsibility to administer this, to dispose of this, to do something with this so that the concept of generosity has a much

different meaning. And I could see that in this particular because of my relationship to the person I knew. I know what the
assets are, I know what had been done with them, I know what
spiritual relationships were with two members of the family
before she reached the point where she was completely help-
less, that dream activity was largely that of visits from her sister and her mother. Mother had been dead a half century, sister had been dead thirty years, but they were both inviting her
to join them which said to me, "take note that she's aware that
the end is not far away."[10]

Tom attempted to integrate his own understanding of spirituality with his teaching. Whenever he encountered an idea growing out
of his experience, he began a class talking about what that new perception was. It created both an opportunity for sharing and also
helped clarify his own position. Spirituality, like theology, arises
from and is carried on in community. Its deepest meaning is experienced there.

Exploring a Common Discourse

Finding ways to come together in this society appears to be more
difficult as the years pass. Common ground or not, we find ever-so-
creative ways to divide ourselves and work at uncommon interests.
But establishing an interconnected community is essential if we are
going to live fully in the wholeness God intends. The Reverend Jesse
Jackson, addressing the 1984 Democratic convention on July 17,
1984, called us to a common and higher ground:

> Our flag is red, white and blue, but our nation is a rainbow—
> red, yellow, brown, black and white—and we're all precious in
> God's sight. America is not like a blanket—one piece of un-
> broken cloth, the same color, the same texture, the same size.
> America is more like a quilt—many patches, many pieces,
> many colors, many sizes, all woven and held together by a
> common thread. . . .
>   Even in our fractured state, all of us count and all of us fit
> somewhere. We have proven that we can survive without each

other. But we have not proven that we can win and progress without each other. We must come together. . . .
We are bound by shared blood and shared sacrifices. We are much too intelligent, much too bound by our Judeo-Christian heritage; much too victimized by racism, sexism, militarism, and anti-Semitism; much too threatened as historical scapegoats to go on divided one from another. We must turn from finger pointing to clasped hands. We must share our burdens and our joys with each other once again. We must turn to each other and not on each other and choose higher ground.[11]

In the previous chapter, we highlighted the strengths of the African American community and its mediating institutions—the church, the school, and the family. These same institutions have been sources for providing mediation across other racial and ethnic communities—in turn to establish interconnected activities in the broader society. This is especially the case in the African American church in terms of its ecumenical outreach. Black ecumenism has been an important means of creating an interconnected community.

The Fraternal Council of Negro Churches, founded in 1934 by the African Methodist Episcopal bishop, Reverdy C. Ransom, remained for years a "significant lobby for the social, economic and political interests of the black church constituency—which is to say, the whole of the African American community."[12] The National Council of Churches and the Southern Christian Leadership Conference have served the purpose of promoting and facilitating interdenominational and interracial activities for the common good of the whole of society. Others should be mentioned, like the National Black Evangelical Association and the Congress of National Black Churches, the latter of which was founded by the African Methodist Episcopal bishop John Hurst Adams (identified previously). Many of these ecumenical groups have attempted to foster broader community involvement in addressing social problems and concerns. Some have "reclaimed the historic liberation motif of the black Church . . . with its dual emphasis on spirituality and social change."[13]

One specific program that has been empowering in our city and other urban areas across this country is the Atlantans Building for Leadership Empowerment (ABLE) initiative. ABLE is the largest religiously based, Atlanta metrowide, multiracial, and interdenominational organization designed to deal not only with "symptoms" in our city, but with the causes of crime, violence, poverty, and racism. The origin of this program comes from the Industrial Areas Foundation (IAF), a grassroots community organizing group, more than fifty years old, whose goal is "to empower the powerless by training leaders and building broad-based, autonomous community organizations so poor and working class citizens can change the economic and political structures that affect their lives."

ABLE has involved approximately two thousand individuals representing forty congregations in the Atlanta area, in creating an "action agenda" for solving community-based problems. The IAF network has forty grassroots citizens' organizations in fourteen states. The Atlanta initiative, or ABLE, is in the early stages of development, but the preliminary indication is it that will be successful. Chiefly, ABLE has been organized to address the effects and causes of poverty in our city. This ecumenical movement has great support across our city.

The Industrial Areas Foundation has an important track record of success. In Los Angeles, groups started by the IAF created a fifteen-million-dollar program to help at-risk youth. In Hudson County, New Jersey, a related group pushed the state to clean up thirty-five waste sites and persuaded local police to double their patrols. Atlanta's ABLE intends to impact its community in similar ways.

ABLE is an example of one of the ways in which we can create an interconnected community in urban areas. The rural setting has great possibilities also.

Developing Leaders, Building Communities: Responding to a Rural Challenge[14]

Rural situations present some peculiar challenges for programs of leadership development. Circumstances of disadvantage, economic impoverishment, and lack of fundamental social services appear larger and more burdensome in those communities. Black urban churches have participated in government-funded programs at a higher rate. Lincoln and Mamiya have surmised that "lack of knowledge and technique of applying to such programs and the absentee pastorate contribute to lower rates for rural churches."[15]

In many rural settings, much of the leadership to initiate and effect sharing and serving the common welfare continues to come from the churches. Interdenominational Theological Center (ITC) has an ongoing commitment to preparing persons for effective ministry in all communities. It has a special interest and would welcome partners who would join in identifying, developing, and nurturing strong leadership to respond to the needs of rural communities.

In 1991, ITC received a grant from the Kellogg Foundation to develop a pilot project. Among its intended goals, the project was designed to strengthen leadership/service activities of persons in congregations and communities in six southeastern states, to encourage and enhance their participation in community affairs, and ultimately to make a positive impact on those communities.

The anticipated outcomes were realized. Emerging and potential leaders were identified, and they participated in training programs. These programs assisted participants to develop and improve their skills in working with groups, increase their understanding of the community-development process, learn more about their communities, and develop plans and carry out strategies for interventions to improve their common life. New courses were developed, and these have strengthened ITC's capacity to prepare its graduates for the increasingly complex and challenging situations they will encounter.

Above and beyond product outcomes, the following were noted:

- Project participants, especially those in the training programs, discovered that they, too—"ordinary people"— had the potential and could make significant contributions to the life to their community.
- Persons discovered their capacity for shared leadership.
- The process attracted and brought people not previously invited to the table.
- Persons discovered the values of clustering and networking.

- Participants learned how to recognize, respond to, and work with pre-existing structures.
- Partnerships between church and community and clergy and laity, ecumenical ventures among churches, a vision of and a commitment to a life together in communities can only improve the commonweal of all citizens.

The project confirmed what participants are continuing to learn: that communities are held together, made safe and hospitable by their internal relationships. These relationships grow out of mutual and communal sharing and support of values and experiences. Relationships are established and grow through shared crisis, hurt, and suffering. Communities are strengthened through those structures that help people to relate, person-to-person, as whole selves in a commitment to and involvement of those things that affect and touch them all. Persons of faith who share their vision of loving and just communities call others to work with them to realize such a vision and find partners and allies who enable them to discover their hidden wholeness.

Finally, the establishment of an interconnected community must begin with the local congregation. The individual church in a specific community is the natural place to start. Discovering hidden wholeness individually and, more importantly, in community is the theme of this text. The spirituality we advocate is most certainly ascertained in the local parish setting.

Among other things, the individual community of faith provides three necessary functions: nurture, operations, and witness. The worship, Christian education, and congregational care of the church's members are central to the nurturing function of each ministry setting. Group decision making, the use of the facilities, and the gathering of financial resources are part of the operational function in the congregation. Witness involves the church in social outreach, evangelism, and advocacy. These three functions (Nurture, Operations, and Witness) thrust the parish into the present (NOW) of everyday life. These important arenas provide opportunity for creative pastoral and lay leadership to empower people through a liberating spirituality.

Vision and Liberating Social Transformation

James A. Forbes Jr. observes that "Conversations about social transformation really begin to be significant when the people discussing the issue speak specifically about the vision that inspires hope; when they articulate the programmatic thrust they propose; and when they describe the source of power and sustenance available to those who commit themselves to the implementation of world changing plans."[16]

A good vision is clear when you can talk to others about it, and you and they can respond to its promptings. It must be consonant with your deeply held personal convictions and values. It is always about relationship and service to others for communal benefit. It is about discovering our hidden wholeness, the hope to be human. This hope cannot be apart from others. For every good vision has implications for us as individuals, as social beings who exist in relationships in organizations and communities, and as persons in societies who share a common humanity in the world.

One of the Greek words for power is "*dunamis*"—explosive power, dynamite. Souls can only receive the power as they are open to encountering God, the source of this power. The God who makes this power available to us challenges us to reflect carefully and critically on the choices we have for its use. This power is available to those who would seek to discover and affirm that a significant recognition of our hidden wholeness is acknowledging our kinship with others. Its proper use is engaging in those actions and activities that constantly affirm our common humanity.

There are some fundamental elements in a process for effecting change in existing situations, for a vision without action may be just a dream, a figment of one's imagination. Engaging in tasks that are not guided by a vision is to be stuck with drudgery. These elements are included in a process cycle. It is important to note that one might start at any point, but must proceed to complete the circle if one expects to observe any transformation.

The cycle is based on the premise that every group of persons engaging in meaningful action for social transformation invites its members:

- To explore and discover their identity and giftedness (to be persons is to have gifts to share).
- To affirm their purpose for existence.
- To discern and develop a shared vision that seeks to respond to people with hidden hurts, and hidden people with hurts, in their communities.
- To take an environmental scan to determine the possibilities of response, given their own values, the resources they share, and the alliances they are able to form.
- To commit themselves to goals that are specific, attainable, and measurable.
- To develop programmatic responses relative to those goals.
- To engage in action, constantly evaluating progress toward agreed goals.
- To note missed opportunities, to learn from mistakes, and always to celebrate victories.
- To make occasions for reflection on those moments of the encounter of God's presence and acknowledge the renewed call to a liberating spirituality.

We offer this model as one way in which those who seek to discover the hidden wholeness may do so. It invites engagement in purposeful and meaningful activity and yet creates space to be aware of the movement of the spirit in life.

Responding to the Challenge

Our exploration into spirituality has been challenging for us, both as ministers and as seminary professors. We have discovered a deeper level of meaning in our practice of ministry as we have engaged in this examination. We hope this text provides a similar challenge.

The liberating aspects of spirituality and their relation to African and African American religiosity have been offered in our exploration. The shapes, continuities, sources, and conventions of African and African American spirituality were provided. The reality of our present society and its connection to a "world disenchanted" has been presented. The generative ways in which the black community, church, school, and family have responded to social realities of American society were given in this examination. Finally, our reaffirmation of God's calling to obedience and an interconnected community was declared with enthusiasm.

While we challenged you with definitional, historical, sociological, and theological ideas for your reflection and action, we pointed to congregations and leaders who model the spirituality we suggest. We have shared stories of persons who make all this real for us as we attempt to teach and practice ministry. We trust that your encounter with this text will lead you and others to greater reflection and dedicated action. We hope your ministry and those who work with you will experience the beauty of the hidden wholeness.

Vision as Challenge: Emily's Letter from Prison[17]

I sit back and wonder what it would be like to live in the days when there was no pollution, no guns, no gangs, no heavy drugs, and no fear to walk around. What would it be like? You wouldn't have to worry about getting shot while "kicking it" at a party or just sitting at a bus stop. You wouldn't have to worry about someone selling your kids drugs, you wouldn't have to worry about what colors you could wear in what part of town.

What's this world coming to? It seems like no one even cares anymore. As I watch the news, I see that another person has been killed. There was another oil spill, or we're over in some other country getting ready to go to war and willing to kill thousands or even millions of innocent people over some stupid reason.

Almost every night I sit and cry and wonder why we are the way we are. I'm only sixteen and I'm scared to do anything anymore, with everything that's going on out there. And now that I know how vulnerable people really are to the problems in this world today, it makes it only scarier. I never realized how weak people really are. They'll go out and shoot someone to show

how powerful they are, but they don't realize it's not them, it's the gun. It doesn't take a genius to be able to pull a trigger. All we're doing is showing how weak we really are. It takes strength to be able to turn a temptation down. We don't realize that we're killing our own race, the human race. Don't you want to live and watch your kids grow up in a safe and secure world?

Sometimes I'm so scared to go out into the world because there's no feel of safety. This is my first time being locked up and I always tell myself, "When I get out I'm never coming back," and the there's times I think that when I get out, I should mess up so I can come back here. In a way when I think about it, this place makes me feel safe, but even in today's world, police don't even "Serve and Protect." They beat someone and get away with it. You can't even trust a person who's supposed to help you. To me that's very sad. Think about it! Do you want your kids to grow up in a place like this?

I know this essay won't make a difference in this world; no essay like this ever has, and probably never will. I just want to know that someone out there will read it and say, "You know what, she's right."

Take a chance, try to make a change. After all, it needs to end somewhere.

Questions for Reflection and Action

1. How can the Christian community become a clearer sign and witness to the wholeness that we believe God intends for the human family?

2. Do you believe, as the spiritual asserts, that "He's got the whole world in his hands?" Why do you dare to believe that in the light of the present realities in the world? In what ways are you and others working to make that affirmation believable?

3. Read again Luke 4:14–30. Note particularly verses 18–21. What does it mean "to proclaim release to the captives" today? Create your vision of the just society for which we confidently strive. What would it look like? How may we work for it?

4. What are two specific programs or ministry activities that you and others might attempt to initiate over the next two years? Which would model a liberating spirituality?

5. What changes in your life need to occur if you, your family, and those you influence at your church *decide* to live a life uncovering the hidden wholeness?

Exercises in a Spirituality of Hidden Wholeness

Rationale for the Exercises

It has been said that education should not be a preparation for life; it should be life. The authors of this book maintain that one should not prepare for spirituality, one should practice it.

Two stories will emphasize the point: "A group of students begged a famous novelist to give them a lecture on how to become writers. The great author began with 'How many of you really intend to be writers?' All hands were raised. 'In that case, there is no point in my talking. My advice to you is, go home and write, write, write.' With that, he returned his notes to his pocket and left the room."[1]

Second, John Wesley, founder of the Methodist Church, records the following conversation he had with Peter Böhler about faith and preaching: "I asked Böhler whether he thought I should leave it off or not [preaching]. He answered, 'By no means.' I asked, 'But what can I preach?' He said, 'Preach faith *till* you have it, and then *because* you have it you will preach faith.' "[2]

Growth in the Christian attributes of love and prayer involves us in a psychospiritual-educational process. The reason why exercises and questions are so important in this text is because we believe that education and spirituality are at the center of life. The philosophy of education represented here is one that includes action-reflection, liberation theology, storytelling, and social action.

The exercises suggested herein fit within the context of these educational practices. It was Anthony de Mello, himself an internationally acclaimed writer and practitioner of spirituality in our lifetime, who stated that he could never write a finished theology of spirituality. All he could do was develop poems, stories, exercises, and epigrams.

These exercises are designed for individual and group use. You are encouraged to utilize them as you and others discover the hidden wholeness. Develop a plan for yourself and others that takes seriously time and space for the engagement of these exercises. You may choose to covenant with others for this exploration. Where there is agreement for this, a similar commitment of time and space should be made. Note and provide other needs for group activities. These may include pencils, markers, three-by-five cards, papers, and/or newsprint. These exercises are just that, but we hope that they may also become for you and others a means of enriching your spiritual journey.

A. Exercise in Awareness

- Have as quiet an environment as possible. Turn off the radio and television.
- Let go of all tension and uptightness. Think relaxation in your legs and arms.
- Allow yourself to feel at home in your seat.
- Close your eyes so as to completely eliminate all visual images.
- Slow down your breathing and create peaceful thoughts.
- Participate in the following meditation.

NOTE: This exercise in *Awareness* may be considered preliminary to the other exercises that follow. You are encouraged to develop this routine.

B. The Process of Meditation

As you attempt spiritually to separate yourself from the false self, you are encouraged to stand back from yourself, to observe yourself. We are closely tied to ourselves—bodies, jobs, gender, color or pigment, and culture. So tied, it is very difficult to be released. Persons are so involved that they are unable to let things go and develop the observer. The observer is the self—the real self. We are slaves to ourselves and only become aware when we stand back and watch ourselves. A good actor is the actor who is not so tied up with the past that he or she becomes the past. The good actor is the person who is able to watch him/herself act. To act from the hidden wholeness as an individual is to act from out of a sacred depth.

As you relax, say to yourself: "I am not my body; I am that which observes my body. I am not my feelings; I watch my feelings. I am not my thoughts; I observe my thoughts as they float by. I am consciousness, pure light, and awareness." The journey to the hidden wholeness, spirituality, and/or the Christ is awareness.

Just as you have stepped aside for critical purposes to look at yourself, now you must synthesize your consciousness and your body, mind, and emotions by saying, "I am not my body, mind, and emotions, but I see them and am the depth of them. I am them."

NOTE: You are now ready to explore any of the questions suggested at the end of each chapter in this book. It is recommended that you follow this practice at the end of each session of the exercises.

Meditation to Show How the Christ is in the Center
of Community or Personal Meditation

- Place a chair in the center of the room.
- Relax with your feet flat on the floor.
- Envision the Christ in the chair.
- Ask Jesus for what you need and want.
- See Christ Jesus in your mind's eye as the Savior comes and stands near you, touches your shoulder, and says, "It is so. You have your need."

Where this is a group activity, the leader may play the role of the Christ.

You may proceed as suggested at the end of Exercise A to explore the reflection questions.

C. Meditation in Bringing Together the Opposites

Note: This is best done as a group exercise. Proceed as follows:

- Place ten chairs in a row. The persons in Group B sit in the chairs and the persons in Group A stand behind them.
- Let persons in Group A represent Jesus and minister to (massage) the ones sitting in the chairs.
- Change places; Group A will now sit and Group B will stand and repeat the exercise.

This exercise shows that the power of God breaks through dualities. When the polarities (Group A and Group B) come together and Christ the Savior has become flesh and dwells among us, the incarnation has come. The dualism comes in community and is broken in community.

D. Meditation on Prayer

- This is a group exercise for participants to engage in a prayer where only the posture or movement of the body is in prayer. One might be prostrate on the floor, one might steeple the hands. Words are not spoken.
- Then go into the groaning prayer, allowing the body to sigh and groan its prayer to God. Move into a mantra, repeating the word "Jesus" over and over again.
- Ask participants to briefly share at the end of the activities, how the experienced these several postures.

E. Meditation on African Myths and Stories

You will need to obtain a copy of Ulli Beier, ed., *The Origin of Life and Death: African Creation Myths* (London: Heinemann, 1966).

- Ask one of the group participants to read the selected story.
- Where possible, the playing of an African flute will enhance the experience.
- Center the mind and discuss the meaning of the myth for you.

F. Meditation on Symbols from Africa

For this exercise, you will need to find music with African drums.

- Listen to the African drumbeat as the music is played on your cassette or CD player.
- Use the book *The Healing Drum: African Wisdom Teachings* by Yaya Diallo and Mitchell Hall (Rochester, Vt.: Destiny Books, 1989) to enhance your appreciation of its significance.
- Afterwards, ask participants to discuss their feelings on listening to the music of the drumbeats.

G. Meditation on Great Leaders

- Place a picture of Martin Luther King Jr. on a table.
- Play "Precious Lord, Take My Hand."
- Then have someone read from page 75.
- Discuss some questions developed beforehand to help participants share their feelings of the significance and greatness of Dr. King.

You may choose to develop similar exercises with other great persons of your choice.

H. Meditation on Purging—
The Wilderness—Catharsis

- Ask participants to develop a list of blockages that have kept them from experiencing the depth or true flow of hidden wholeness within themselves, others, culture, or the universe. Use the insights discussed in this book.
- Afterwards, ask participants to share their responses.
- Seek to develop some consensus for bringing this activity to closure.

I. Exercise in the Use of a Mantra

- Have as quiet an environment as possible. Turn off the radio and television.
- Let go of all tension and uptightness. Think relaxation in your legs and arms.
- Allow yourself to feel at home in your seat.
- Close your eyes so as to completely eliminate all visual images.
- Listen for noise in the room or outside of the room. Person or persons are encouraged to "go with the beat." This helps the person(s) to "be."

"Be still and know that I am God."
"Be still and know that I am"
"Be still and know that I"
"Be still and know that"
"Be still and know"
"Be still"
"Be"
"Be"
"Be"

This exercise helps the group to overcome existing noises and prepares the mind for further meditation. You may conclude this exercise with no further activity.

Suggestions for Using the Questions for Reflection and Action

This text is written for use by individuals as well as by persons in group settings: in congregations, seminaries, and other institutions. The reflection and discussion questions at the end of each chapter will facilitate this process. You and others are encouraged to use this opportunity as you and they engage in a journey toward wholeness.

You may choose to explore the questions by yourself or in company with others. It will be useful to keep a reflection journal. This is different from a diary. In a reflection journal, you are invited to record significant experiences or events in your life. In recording them, you may move between experiences, feelings, and reflections that help to provide some understanding, make some sense or meaning of those experiences; they may affect your faith. These experiences and reflections may also lead to some purposeful engagement.

If you are using these questions in a group setting, the group may wish to select a moderator whose job will be to facilitate the process, and a recorder who will keep notes of your findings and decisions that you make.

The following are some ongoing questions that you may wish to consider:

- How does this experience or event help me to discern the presence or absence of God in my life?
- What insights do these events/experiences offer into myself as a person of faith?

- How do they help me to respond to and with others as persons who seek to be faithful and obedient to the claims of God on my life in community?

We invite you and others to consider seriously this useful comment as you engage in this process: "Eventful education involves our *engagement* in the event. Events transform lives only as people enter into them and allow their imagination to be filled with its possibilities, their relationships with its expectations, and their practices with its values. . . . A lack of engagement reduces us to the passivity of observation without calling us to commitment or transformation."[1]

African American Male Bonding: The Million Man March

As a final thought, we would like to share with you our reflections on the 1995 Million Man March. We invite you and others to consider this significant event as a transforming experience for the African American community and the nation as a whole.

The Million Man March evoked much commentary when it was announced and when it took place. It continues to draw comments. Much has been said and written about its leadership and its leader, the ever-controversial Louis Farrakhan. There was dispute about its numbers—there weren't one million there! It is interesting to observe that the media even ventured to suggest that there was a spirituality to the experience that defied expression in words. Television camera operators confessed that "the TV doesn't do spiritual real well."

Whatever can be said about the event, there was a continuing consensus that it expressed a will to affirm a sense of connectedness, solidarity, and community, especially among African American males. A spirit of love and a commitment to togetherness, oneness, and unity seemed to prevail. As Jesse Jackson observed, it was "beautiful to see the rejected stones stand up, become the cornerstones of a new spiritual order."

It is the spirituality of the experience to which we wish to allude. There was a sense that persons were drawn together by a spirit greater than themselves or the leaders or personalities who were principal actors. Our colleague and academic dean Calvin S. Morris was present at the event in 1995 and at the earlier one in 1963.

We invited him to reflect particularly on the 1995 event. We believe that the event and his remarks illustrate several aspects of the spirituality of the African American experience of which we have been writing.

There is a passage of scripture that speaks of witnesses coming from the North and from the South, from the East and from the West. . . . This is how I saw this panoply of the generations of African Americans who gathered in Washington for the Million Man March. There were sons and fathers, and their fathers and sons; grandfathers; four generations of people. There was the nuclear family and the extended family of persons related indirectly, all African American. People carrying folk on their shoulders; men walking hand in hand; a huge crowd of people. I sensed a "parting of the waters" and I was passing through with that throng. There were greetings of friends and neighbors, fellows on a journey, as they hailed one another with: "Brother, glad to see you." "Isn't this a wonderful day?" It seemed to express not only family solidarity, but a oneness in the human family.

And women, our sisters, were there also, with their children, many of them sons. All seemed to be caught up in this congregation of maleness. I saw men, not related to the kids but connecting with these children. There was a sense of identity: that we were all related, of the same stock and kind. As I made my way to the Mall with others, there were the elders on their stoops and from their windows, beaming at what they saw! "Isn't this wonderful?" they exclaimed. You could see the pride in the eyes of those who beheld this movement of men.

I had gone to Washington for the meeting of a board of which I am a member. I had not planned to go to the march. But as time wore on and the masses of men started assembling, I grew restless, I could not stay away. I told one of my friends at the board meeting, "I've got to go!" And so I responded, as if drawn by a spirit I could not readily identify.

The presence of that great assemblage of men—black men, often maligned and put down, demeaned, and humiliated— seemed to say, "We are still here!" "While not perceived by the media as significant, we've always been here. We're here with our fathers and our sons, our nephews, and our uncles. We're here with our grandfathers, our sons, our family, our churches, our communities." It seemed to be one great "cloud of wit-

nesses," African Americans, to be sure, but people whose personhood found affirmation in the heart of God, God's people.
   As I reflect on the March on Washington in 1963 and the Million Man March of the fall of 1995, the 1995 event was more sobering. In 1963 there seemed to be a sense of freedom in the air. In 1995 there was a steely determination, not only of survival, but to move forward. This march was called out of a period of deep distress. The distress evident in 1963 prompted a challenge to confrontation and engagement. The Million Man March had a less-positive determination. There was an underlying anomie. The coming together was to discover bonding and togetherness in a massive way, in a movement. At both events, the official Washington response was the same: fear and apprehension. The city was abandoned.[1]

   Perhaps any spirituality that could be discerned in the Million Man March contained the elements witness and prophecy. There are two related impulses to witness: self-justification and judgment. Public witness is a necessary ritual in a cathartic process. Here, it was a statement that was necessary for black males to make. It was a purging of self-doubt that suggested their coming together was not possible. The participants made simultaneous discovery that set in motion, for them, both healing and bonding.
   The statement of that vast assembly was a judgment on as well as a prophecy to a nation, an uncaring and corrupt society that writes off generations of the disadvantaged and marginalized by a persistent indifference to their plight. By their presence in Washington, in October 1995, African American males, with one prophetic voice, declared a loud "No" to all the false images of their own persons. They challenged a nation to recognize its humanity by engaging in a necessary introspection. This movement in is also a movement out and on to the discovery of the hidden wholeness.

Notes

Preface

1. Dag Hammarskjöld, *Markings,* trans. Leif Sjöberg and W. H. Auden (Londen: Faber and Faber, 1964).

Introduction

1. William H. Parker, "Tell Me the Stories of Jesus," in the *United Methodist Hymnal* (Nashville, Tenn.: United Methodist Publishing House, 1989), 277.

2. Thomas Toke Lynch, "Dismiss Me Not Thy Service, Lord," in the *Methodist Hymn Book* (London: Methodist Conference Office, 1954), 580.

3. John Henry Newman, "Lead, Kindly Light," in *American Service Hymnal* (Nashville, Tenn.: John T. Benson Publishing Co., 1968), 392.

4. F. Bland Tucker, "Awake, O Sleeper," *United Methodist Hymnal,* 551.

1. "Breaking through the Pavement"

1. Howard Thurman, *For the Inward Journey* (Richmond, Ind.: Friends United Press, 1984), 64.

2. "The Measure of a Man," in *Complete Speaker's and Toastmaster's Library: Speech Openers and Closers,* ed. Jacob M. Braude (Englewood Cliffs, N.J.: Prentice-Hall, 1965), 44.

3. Thurman, *For the Inward Journey,* x.

4. Samuel Amirtham, ed., *Spiritual Formation in Theological Education: An Invitation to Participate* (Geneva, Switz.: World Council of Churches, 1987), 3.

5. Ibid., 7.

6. Ibid., 10.

7. Matthew Fox, *Original Blessing* (Santa Fe, N.M.: Bean & Co., 1983), 39.

8. Robert McAfee Brown, *Spirituality and Liberation: Overcoming the Great Fallacy* (Philadelphia: Westminster Press, 1988), 27–30.

9. Ibid., 116–19.

10. Ibid., 121–24.

11. Gustavo Gutiérrez, *We Drink from Our Own Wells* (Maryknoll, N.Y.: Orbis Books, 1984), 128.

12. Clifford Geertz, *The Interpretation of Cultures* (New York: Basic Books, 1973).

13. Gayraud Wilmore, *Black Religion and Black Radicalism* (Maryknoll, N.Y.: Orbis Books, 1983), ix.

14. Wallace Charles Smith, *The Church in the Life of the Black Family* (Valley Forge, Pa.: Judson Press, 1985), 41.

15. Gayraud S. Wilmore, "Spirituality and Social Transformation as the Vocation of the Black Church," in *Churches in Struggle: Liberation Theologies and Social Change in North America*, ed. William K. Tabb (New York: Monthly Review Press, 1986), 240.

2. "No Other Tale to Tell"

1. James Baldwin, "Sonny's Blues," in *Going to Meet the Man* (London: Corgi Books, 1967), 123.

2. James Baldwin, "Interview with Inmates at Riker's Island Prison in New York," *Essence* (June 1976), 80.

3. James Baldwin, *Notes of a Native Son* (New York: Bantam Books, 1955), 71.

4. See, for example, Maulana Karenga, *Introduction to Black Studies* (Los Angeles: Kawaida Publications, 1982); Katie G. Cannon, *Black Womanist Ethics* (Atlanta: Scholars Press, 1988); Jacquelyn Grant, *White Women's Christ and Black Women's Jesus: Feminist Christology and Womanist Response* (Atlanta: Scholars Press, 1989); Molefi Kefe Asante and Kariamu Welsh Asante, *African Culture: Rhythms of Unity* (Westport, Conn.: Greenwood Press, 1985); C. Eric Lincoln and Lawrence H. Mamiya, *The Black Church in the African American Experience* (Durham, N.C.: Duke University Press, 1990); Emilie M. Townes, ed., *A Troubling in My Soul: Womanist Perspectives on Evil and Suffering* (New York: Orbis Books, 1993); and Theophus H. Smith, *Conjuring Culture: Biblical Formulations of Black America* (New York: Oxford University Press, 1994). Among the earlier scholars in this field were James H. Cone, *Black Theology and Black Power* (New York: Seabury Press, 1969); J. Deotis Roberts, *Liberation and Reconciliation* (Philadelphia: Westminster, 1971); and

Gayraud Wilmore, *Black Religion and Black Radicalism* (Maryknoll, N.Y.: Orbis Books, 1983).

5. Charles H. Long, *Significations: Signs, Symbols, and Images in the Interpretation of Religion* (Philadelphia: Fortress Press, 1986), 149.

6. Lincoln and Mamiya, *The Black Church*, xii.

7. Henry Louis Gates Jr., "The Face and Voice of Blackness," in *Facing History: The Black Image in American Art, 1710–1940*, ed. Guy C. McElroy (San Francisco: Bedford Arts, 1990), xxix.

8. Henry Louis Gates Jr., *Loose Canons: Notes on the Culture Wars* (New York: Oxford University Press, 1992), xvii.

9. Ibid.

10. Cornel West, *Race Matters* (Boston: Beacon Press, 1993), 11.

11. Amirtham, *Spiritual Formation*, 3.

12. Howard Thurman, *Disciplines of the Spirit* (Richmond, Ind.: Friends United Press, 1987), 9.

13. Kofi Asare Opoku, *West African Traditional Religion* (Jurong, Singapore: FEP International Private Ltd., 1978), 9.

14. Ibid., 10–11.

15. West, *Race Matters*, 5.

16. H. Wheeler Robinson, "Hebrew Psychology," in *The People and the Book*, ed. A. S. Peake (Oxford: The Clarendon Press, 1925), 362.

17. Peter K. Sarpong, "Everyday Tribal Spirituality," *International Christian Digest* 1 (May 1988): 24–26.

18. John S. Mbiti, *African Religions and Philosophy* (New York: Praeger, 1969), 1.

19. See, for example, the works of Leonard E. Barrett, *Soul-Force: African Heritage in Afro-American Religion* (New York: Anchor/Doubleday, 1974); John W. Blassingame, ed., *Slave Testimony: Two Centuries of Letters, Speeches, Interviews, and Autobiographies* (Baton Rouge: Louisiana State University Press, 1977); Albert J. Raboteau, *Slave Religion: The "Invisible Institution" in the Antebellum South* (New York: Oxford University Press, 1978); Asante and Asante, *African Culture;* Jamie Phelps, "Black Spirituality," in *Spiritual Traditions for the Contemporary Church*, ed. Robin Maas and Gabriel O'Donnell (Nashville, Tenn.: Abingdon Press, 1990); Smith, *Conjuring Culture*; and Peter J. Paris, *The Spirituality of African Peoples: The Search for a Common Moral Discourse* (Minneapolis: Fortress Press, 1995).

20. Mervyn Alleyne, *Roots of Jamaican Culture* (London: Pluto Press, 1988), 17.

21. Ibid., 23.

22. Sarpong, "Everyday Tribal Spirituality," 23.

23. John S. Mbiti, "Theological Impotence and the Universality of

the Church," in *Mission Trends*, ed. Gerald H. Anderson and Thomas F. Stransky (New York: Paulist Press, 1976), 8.

24. Paris, *The Spirituality of African Peoples*, 27.

25. Ibid., 25.

26. Ibid., 26. See also Ndugu G. B. T'Ofori-Atta, "Eight Stages in the Holistic Life Cycle 'In the Hood' of Traditional African Religion," *Journal of the Interdenominational Theological Center* 23 (Spring 1996): 81–120. In this essay, T'Ofori-Atta explores how these understandings of the African spiritual cosmos inform the life cycle and ultimately the spirituality of African peoples.

27. Paris, *The Spirituality of African Peoples*, 35.

28. Malidoma Patrice Somé, *Of Water and the Spirit: Ritual, Magic and Initiation in the Life of an African Shaman* (New York: Penguin Books, 1994).

29. Ibid., 70–71.

30. Ibid., 66.

31. Ibid., 52.

32. Ibid., 83.

33. Robin Maas and Gabriel O'Donnell, eds. *Spiritual Traditions for the Contemporary Church* (Nashville, Tenn.: Abingdon Press, 1990), 332.

34. Theophus H. Smith, "The Spirituality of Afro-American Traditions," in *Christian Spirituality: Post Reformation and Modern*, ed. Louis Dupre and Don E. Saliers (New York: Crossroad, 1991), 372.

35. Jacqueline P. Butler, "Of Kindred Minds: The Ties That Bind," in *Cultural Competence for Evaluators*, ed. Mario A. Orlandi, Raymond Weston, and Leonard G. Epstein (Rockville, Md.: U.S. Department of Health and Human Services, 1992), 30–31.

36. Raboteau, *Slave Religion*, 88.

37. Charles H. Perdue Jr., Thomas E. Barden, and Robert K. Phillips, eds., *Weevils in the Wheat: Interviews with Virginia Ex-Slaves* (Charlottesville: University of Virginia Press, 1994), 184.

38. Robert Michael Franklin, class presentation (Atlanta: Interdenominational Theological Center, 1992).

39. Long, *Significations*, 152.

40. Ibid.

41. Smith, "The Spirituality of Afro-American Traditions," 374.

42. Wardell J. Payne, ed., *Directory of African American Religious Bodies* (Washington, D.C.: Howard University Press, 1995), 103. See also Aminah Beverly McCloud, *African American Islam* (New York: Routledge, 1995). McCloud, an Islamic scholar, surveys several Muslim communities in the United States. She seeks to clarify misconcep-

tions that are held about the African American presence in Islam. She proposes further research is needed into African American Islam, which is the largest ethnic component of a rapidly growing religion in the United States.

43. Janice E. Hale, "The Transmission of Faith to Young African American Children," in *The Recovery of the Black Presence: An Interdisciplinary Exploration*, ed. Randall C. Bailey and Jacquelyn Grant (Nashville, Tenn.: Abingdon Press, 1995), 198.

44. Raboteau, *Slave Religion*, 242. See also Riggins R. Earl Jr., *Dark Symbols, Obscure Signs: God, Self and Community in the Slave Mind* (Maryknoll, N.Y.: Orbis Books, 1993). In it Earl examines the problems slaves had in responding to the misrepresentations the masters made of biblical doctrines to justify their treatment of the slaves. He contends that "slaves used different genres of their native religion to counter the negative view of their spiritual and physical nature" (7). They reconstructed the Christian language to shape a new sense of self-affirmation that made them sacred in the sight of God.

45. Smith, *Conjuring Culture*.

46. Ibid., 222.

47. Ibid., 224.

48. Cone, *Black Theology and Black Power*, 35.

49. See, for example, Howard Thurman, *Deep River and the Negro Spiritual Speaks of Life and Death* (Richmond, Ind.: Friends United Press, 1975); Eileen Southern, *The Music of Black Americans* (New York: W. W. Norton, 1971); Eugene Genovese, *Roll, Jordan, Roll: The World the Slaves Made* (New York: Pantheon, 1974); William B. McClain, *Come Sunday: The Liturgy of Zion* (Nashville, Tenn.: Abingdon Press, 1990); Jon Michael Spencer, *Protest and Praise: Sacred Music of Black Religion* (Minneapolis: Fortress Press, 1990); James H. Cone, *The Spirituals and the Blues* (New York: Orbis Books, 1991); Melva W. Costen and Darius L. Swann, eds., *The Black Christian Worship Experience*, rev. ed., vol. 4, Black Church Scholars Series (Atlanta: ITC Press, 1992); Melva Wilson Costen, *African American Christian Worship* (Nashville, Tenn.: Abingdon Press, 1994).

50. See, for example, Henry H. Mitchell, *Black Preaching* (Philadelphia: Lippincott, 1970); Henry H. Mitchell, *Celebration and Experience in Preaching* (Nashville, Tenn.: Abingdon Press, 1990); Lincoln and Mamiya, *The Black Church*.

51. W. E. B. DuBois, *The Souls of Black Folk: Essays and Sketches by W. E. Burghardt DuBois* (1903; reprint, New York: Dodd, Mead, 1979), 142.

52. See Martin Luther King Jr., *Stride Toward Freedom: The Mont-*

gomery Story (New York: Harper & Row, 1958); Martin Luther King Jr., *Strength to Love* (New York: Harper & Row, 1963); Lincoln and Mamiya, *The Black Church*.

53. John S. Mbiti, "African Religion," in *The Study of Spirituality*, ed. Cheslyn Jones, Geoffrey Wainwright, and Edward Yarnold (New York: Oxford University Press, 1986), 514.

54. Harold A. Carter, *The Prayer Tradition of Black People* (Valley Forge, Pa.: Judson Press, 1976), 128. See also Lincoln and Mamiya, *The Black Church*, 352. The authors affirmed the practices of "shouting" as it has developed in the African American experience and as it is practiced in African religious rites.

55. James Baldwin, *Just above My Head* (New York: Dell, 1979), 113.

56. Ibid., 244.

57. Molefi Kete Asante, *Afrocentricity* (Trenton, N.J.: Africa World Press, 1988), 74.

58. Franklin, class presentation.

59. Grant S. Shockley, "Black Theology," in *Encyclopedia of Religious Education*, ed. Iris V. Cully and Kendig Brubaker Cully (San Francisco: Harper & Row, 1990), 80.

60. Grant, *White Women's Christ and Black Women's Jesus*, dedication page.

61. Ibid., x.

62. Ibid., 3.

63. Ibid., ix.

3. "Dis Howlin' Wildaness"

1. David T. Shannon, "'An Ante-bellum Sermon': A Resource for an African American Hermeneutic," in *Stony the Road We Trod: African American Biblical Interpretation*, ed. Cain Hope Felder (Minneapolis: Fortress Press, 1991), 105–7.

2. James Weldon Johnson, *God's Trombones: Seven Negro Sermons in Verse* (New York: Penguin Books, 1976), 27–30.

3. James H. Cone, *The Spirituals and the Blues* (New York: Orbis Books, 1991).

4. Marie Augusta Neal, *The Just Demands of the Poor* (New York: Paulist Press, 1987), 101.

5. Ibid., 41–42.

6. William B. Kennedy, "The Ideological Captivity of the Non-Poor," in *Pedagogies for the Non-Poor*, ed. Alice F. Evans, Robert A. Evans, and William B. Kennedy (Maryknoll, N.Y.: Orbis Books, 1987), 232.

7. Paul G. King, Kent Maynard, and David O. Woodyard, *Risking Liberation: Middle Class Powerlessness and Social Heroism* (Atlanta: John Knox Press, 1988), 87.

8. Ibid., 50.

9. Lincoln and Mamiya, *The Black Church*, 237.

10. Cornel West, *Prophecy Deliverance* (Philadelphia: The Westminster Press, 1982), 47.

11. Joseph Barndt, *Dismantling Racism: The Continuing Challenge to White America* (Minneapolis: Augsburg/Fortress Press, 1991), viii.

12. West, *Race Matters*, 4.

13. David H. Swinton, "The Economic Status of African Americans: 'Permanent' Poverty and Inequality," in *The State of Black America*, ed. Janet Dewart (New York: National Urban League, 1991), 29.

14. Manning Marable, "The Rhetoric of Racial Harmony," in *America's Original Sin: A Study Guide on White Racism*, ed. Sojourners (Washington, D.C.: Editor, 1992), 114.

15. Patrick G. Coy, "Conscientious Objection to the Drug War," *Christianity and Crisis* 50 (1990): 245.

16. Marable, "The Rhetoric of Racial Harmony," 114.

17. M. Garlinda Burton, *Never Say Nigger Again! An Antiracism Guide for White Liberals* (Nashville, Tenn.: James C. Winston, 1995). See also C. Eric Lincoln, *Coming through the Fire: Surviving Race and Place in America* (Durham, N.C.: Duke University Press, 1996). Lincoln, the distinguished sociologist and noted scholar of the African American experience, examines the whole issue of race in our society. He argues that since the problem is rooted in the infrastructure of our society, every human response is a racial response, and that we must eventually come to terms with the emerging multicultural nature of our society, in which we acknowledge "no-fault reconciliation" and a mutual recognition of the human endowment that we share.

18. Burton, *Never Say Nigger Again!* 3.

19. Ibid., 84 (emphasis added).

20. Pauli Murray, "Black Theology and Feminist Theology: A Comparative View," in *Black Theology: A Documentary History, 1966–1979*, ed. Gayraud S. Wilmore and James H. Cone (Maryknoll, N.Y.: Orbis Books, 1979), 402.

21. Keith Roberts, *Religion in Sociological Perspective* (New York: Wadsworth, 1995), 313.

22. Murray, "Black Theology and Feminist Theology," 402.

23. Joni Seager and Ann Olson, *Women in the World: An International Atlas* (New York: Simon & Schuster, 1986), 101.

24. Ibid.

25. Ibid., 114.

26. Ibid., 81.

27. Ibid., 7.

28. This tale was presented by Timothy Broughton, a graduate of ITC (1994), as part of a paper for a class that the authors team-taught in the fall of 1992. This is an edited version of that paper.

29. West, *Race Matters*, 14–15.

30. George Stroup, "Revelation," in *Christian Theology: An Introduction to Its Traditions and Tasks*, 2nd ed., rev. and enl., ed. Peter C. Hodgson and Robert H. King (Philadelphia: Fortress Press, 1985), 125.

31. Alexis de Tocqueville, *Democracy in America*, trans. George Lawrence (New York: Doubleday/Anchor Books, 1969).

32. Robert N. Bellah, Richard Madsen, William M. Sullivan, Ann Swidler, and Steven M. Tipton, *Habits of the Heart: Individualism and Commitment in American Life* (Los Angeles: University of California Press, 1985); Robert N. Bellah, Richard Madsen, William M. Sullivan, Ann Swidler, and Steven M. Tipton, *The Good Society* (New York: Vintage Books, 1991).

33. Martin Luther King Jr., "The American Dream," in *A Testament of Hope: The Essential Writings of Martin Luther King, Jr.*, ed. James Melvin Washington (New York: Harper & Row, 1986), 209.

34. Brown, *Spirituality and Liberation*, 27.

35. Dagobert D. Runes, ed., *Dictionary of Philosophy* (Totowa, N.J.: Littlefield, Adams, 1967), 84.

36. Joseph C. Hough Jr. and John B. Cobb Jr., *Christian Identity and Theological Education* (Chico, Calif.: Scholars Press, 1985), 40.

37. Fox, *Original Blessing*, 54.

38. Meredith McGuire, *Religion: The Social Context* (Belmont, Calif.: Wadsworth, 1992), 225.

39. Ibid., 226.

40. Ibid.

41. Ibid., 264.

42. Ibid.

43. Lincoln and Mamiya, *The Black Church*, xi.

44. Peter J. Paris, *The Social Teaching of the Black Churches* (Philadelphia: Fortress Press, 1985), 13.

45. Ibid., 11.

46. Ibid., 10.

47. Ibid.

48. From "A City of Hope, A People of Hope," brochure of Ray of Hope Christian Church, Decatur, Georgia.

49. Jeremiah A. Wright Jr., "Unashamedly Black and Unapologetically Christian," in *African Roots: Towards an Afrocentric Christian Witness*, ed. Michael I. N. Dash, L. Rita Dixon, Darius L. Swann, and Ndugu T'Ofori-Atta (Lithonia, Ga.: SCP/Third World Literature, 1994), 174.

50. Ibid., 178.

51. Ibid., 191.

52. Ibid., 195.

53. Cecil Williams and Rebecca Laird, *No Hiding Place: Empowerment and Recovery for Our Troubled Communities* (New York: HarperCollins, 1992).

54. Ibid., book cover.

4. "In a Single Garment of Destiny"

1. King, "The American Dream," 210.

2. Ibid., 219.

3. Henri J. M. Nouwen, *Lifesigns: Intimacy, Fecundity, and Ecstacy in Christian Perspective* (New York: Doubleday, 1986), 15.

4. West, *Race Matters*, 105.

5. Andrew M. Billingsley, *Climbing Jacob's Ladder: The Enduring Legacy of African-American Families* (New York: Touchstone Books, 1992), 80.

6. West, *Race Matters*, 58.

7. Anne S. Wimberly, interview by authors, fall 1992, Atlanta, Georgia, tape recording.

8. Ibid.

9. Mbiti, *African Religions and Philosophy*, 108.

10. Ibid., 108–9.

11. Billingsley, *Climbing Jacob's Ladder*, 70.

12. Ibid., 71–72.

13. Ibid., 72.

14. Ibid., 73.

15. C. Eric Lincoln, *Race, Religion and the Continuing American Dilemma* (New York: Hill & Wang, 1984), 96.

16. Lincoln and Mamiya, *The Black Church*, 382.

17. Billingsley, *Climbing Jacob's Ladder*, 172.

18. Ibid.

19. Ibid.

20. Lincoln, *Coming through the Fire*, 28.

21. Billingsley, *Climbing Jacob's Ladder*, 94.

22. Ibid., 106.

23. Lincoln, *Race, Religion*, 199.

24. Ibid., 198.

25. Ibid.

26. Ibid., 172.

27. Ibid. See, for example, Yosef ben-Jochannan, *Africa: Mother of Western Civilization* (New York: Alkebu-Ian Books, 1971); Asa G. Hilliard, Larry Williams, and Nia Damali, eds., *The Teachings of Ptah Hotep: The Oldest Book in the World* (Atlanta: Blackwood Press, 1987); Cheikh Anta Diop, *The Cultural Unity of Black Africa: The Domains of Patriarchy and of Matriarchy in Classical Antiquity* (Chicago: Third World Press, 1978); Martin Bernal, *Black Athena: The Afroasiatic Roots of Classical Civilization*, vol. 1 (New Brunswick, N.J.: Rutgers University Press, 1987); Ivan Van Sertima, ed., *The African Presence in Ancient America: They Came Before Columbus* (New York: Random House, 1976); Ivan Van Sertima, ed., *African Presence in Early Asia* (New Brunswick, N.J.: Transaction Books, 1985); Ivan Van Sertima, ed., *African Presence in Early Europe* (New Brunswick, N.J.: Transaction Books, 1992); Charles S. Finch III, *Echoes of the Old Darkland: Themes from the African Eden* (Decatur, Ga.: Khenti, 1993).

28. Billingsley, *Climbing Jacob's Ladder*, 94.

29. Ibid., 106. See also E. Franklin Frazier, *The Negro Family in the United States* (Chicago: University of Chicago Press, 1939). This foundational study explores the concepts and understandings of family as experiences both in the slave period and beyond. He particularly emphasizes bonding relationships between mother and children. This is evident among African Americans today.

30. Lincoln, *Race, Religion*, 328–33.

31. West, *Race Matters*, 43.

32. Ibid., 38.

33. Ibid.

34. Ibid., 40.

35. Ibid., 36.

36. Henri J. M. Nouwen, "Career and Vocation," in *Seeds of Hope: A Henri Nouwen Reader*, ed. Robert Durback (New York: Bantam Books, 1989), 94.

37. Howard Thurman, *Meditations of the Heart* (Richmond, Ind.: Friends United Press, 1976), 86.

38. Jim Wallis, *The Soul of Politics: Beyond "Religious Right" and "Secular Left"* (New York: Harcourt Brace, 1995), xix–xx.

39. Letter from Mamie Hillman, executive director of Empowering Parents for Troubled Times, Inc., to Michael Dash, project director.

40. From "'It Takes a Village': Our Sons and Daughters as Parents," brochure of teen pregnancy and parent symposium, 9 May 1996, Greene County Law Enforcement Center, Greensboro, Georgia.

41. King, "The American Dream," 210.

5. "He's Got the Whole World in His Hands"

1. "He's Got the Whole World in His Hands," *Songs of Zion* (Nashville, Tenn.: Abingdon Press, 1981), 85.

2. Cheryl Kirk-Duggan, "African American Spirituals: Confronting and Exorcising the Evil through Song," in *A Troubling in My Soul: Womanist Perspectives on Evil and Suffering*, ed. Emilie M. Townes (Maryknoll, N.Y.: Orbis Books, 1993), 164.

3. Opoku, *West African Traditional Religion*, 8.

4. Kofi Asare Opoku, "Ancient Wisdom in African Heritage," *International Christian Digest* 4 (May 1988): 34.

5. Ron Nored is a 1989 graduate of Interdenominational Theological Center, Atlanta. He currently pastors in Birmingham, Alabama, and is also executive director of BEAT.

6. Charles Shelby Rooks, *Rainbows and Reality: Selected Writings of the Author* (Atlanta: The ITC Press, 1985), 104.

7. Amirtham, *Spiritual Formation*, 9.

8. Augustine, *The Confessions*, Book. I, in *The Book of Worship* (Nashville, Tenn.: United Methodist Publishing House, 1965), 251.

9. King, "The American Dream," 210.

10. Thomas J. Pugh, interview by authors, 1991, Atlanta, tape recording.

11. Jesse Jackson, "The Call of Conscience, the Courage of Conviction," excerpted from address to Democratic Convention, 17 July 1984, *The New York Times*, 18 July 1984, A18.

12. Lincoln and Mamiya, *The Black Church*, 192.

13. Ibid., 193.

14. Michael I. N. Dash, *Story Telling, Story Listening, Story Making: Final Report to the Kellogg Foundation* (Atlanta: Interdenominational Theological Center, 1995).

15. Lincoln and Mamiya, *The Black Church*, 363.

16. James A. Forbes Jr., "Social Transformation," in *Living with Apocalypse: Spiritual Resources for Social Compassion*, ed. Tilden H. Edwards (San Francisco: Harper & Row, 1984), 41.

17. Asha Mawusi Bell, class presentation (Atlanta: Interdenominational Theological Center, spring 1996).

Appendix 1: Exercises in a Spirituality of Hidden Wholeness

1. One of the authors was enrolled in a class in which this story was told. It is being recounted from memory. No further details of its source can be recalled.

2. Nehemiah Curnock, ed., *The Journal of John Wesley,* standard ed., vol. 1 (New York: Eaton and Mains, 1909), 442.

Appendix 2: Suggestions for Using the Questions for Reflection and Action

1. Charles R. Foster, *The Future of Christian Education: Educating Congregations* (Nashville, Tenn.: Abingdon Press, 1994), 48.

Appendix 3: African American Male Bonding

1. Calvin S. Morris, interview by authors, 28 June 1996, Interdenominational Theological Center, Atlanta, Georgia.

Selected Bibliography

Alleyne, Mervyn. *Roots of Jamaican Culture*. London: Pluto Press, 1988.

Amirtham, Samuel, ed. *Spiritual Formation in Theological Education: An Invitation to Participate*. Geneva, Switz.: World Council of Churches, 1987.

Asante, Molefi Kete. *Afrocentricity*. Trenton, N.J.: Africa World Press, 1988.

Asante, Molefi Kete, and Kariamu Welsh Asante, *African Culture: Rhythms of Unity*. Westport, Conn.: Greenwood Press, 1985.

Augustine. *The Confessions*, Book I. In *The Book of Worship*. Nashville, Tenn.: United Methodist Publishing House, 1965.

Baldwin, James. *Just Above My Head*. New York: Dell, 1979.

———. *Notes of a Native Son*. New York: Bantam Books, 1955.

———. "Sonny's Blues." In *Going to Meet the Man*. London: Corgi Books, 1967.

Barndt, Joseph. *Dismantling Racism: The Continuing Challenge to White America*. Minneapolis: Augsburg/Fortress Press, 1991.

Barrett, Leonard E., *Soul-Force: African Heritage in Afro-American Religion*. New York: Anchor/Doubleday, 1974.

Beier, Ulli, ed. *The Origin of Life and Death: African Creation Myths*. London: Heinemann, 1966.

Bellah, Robert N., Richard Madsen, William M. Sullivan, Ann Swidler, and Steven M. Tipton. *The Good Society*. New York: Vintage Books, 1991.

———. *Habits of the Heart: Individualism and Commitment in American Life*. Los Angeles: University of California Press, 1985.

Billingsley, Andrew M. *Climbing Jacob's Ladder: The Enduring Legacy of African-American Families*. New York: Touchstone Books, 1992.

Blassingame, John W., ed. *Slave Testimony: Two Centuries of Letters, Speeches, Interviews, and Autobiographies*. Baton Rouge: Louisiana State University Press, 1977.

Braude, Jacob M., ed. *Complete Speaker's and Toastmaster's Library:*

Speech Openers and Closers. Englewood Cliffs, N.J.: Prentice-Hall, 1965.

Brown, Robert McAfee. *Spirituality and Liberation: Overcoming the Great Fallacy.* Philadelphia: Westminster Press, 1988.

Burton, M. Garlinda. *Never Say Nigger Again! An Antiracism Guide for White Liberals.* Nashville, Tenn.: James C. Winston, 1995.

Butler, Jacqueline P. "Of Kindred Minds: The Ties That Bind." In *Cultural Competence for Evaluators,* edited by Mario A. Orlandi, Raymond Weston, and Leonard G. Epstein, 30–31. Rockville, Md.: U.S. Department of Health and Human Services, 1992.

Cannon, Katie G. *Black Womanist Ethics.* Atlanta: Scholars Press, 1988.

Carter, Harold A. *The Prayer Tradition of Black People.* Valley Forge, Pa.: Judson Press, 1976.

Cone, James H. *Black Theology and Black Power.* New York: Seabury Press, 1969.

———. *The Spirituals and the Blues.* New York: Orbis Books, 1991.

Costen, Melva Wilson. *African American Christian Worship.* Nashville, Tenn.: Abingdon Press, 1993.

Costen, Melva W., and Darius L. Swann, eds. *The Black Christian Worship Experience.* Rev. ed. Vol. 4. Black Church Scholars Series. Atlanta: ITC Press, 1992.

Coy, Patrick G. "Conscientious Objection to the Drug War." *Christianity and Crisis* 50 (1990): 243–46.

Dash, Michael I. N. *Story Telling, Story Listening, Story Making: Final Report to the Kellogg Foundation.* Atlanta: Interdenominational Theological Center, 1995.

Diallo, Yaya, and Mitchell Hall. *The Healing Drum: African Wisdom Teachings.* Rochester, Vt.: Destiny Books, 1989.

DuBois, W. E. B. *The Souls of Black Folk: Essays and Sketches by W. E. Burghardt DuBois,* 1903. Reprint, New York: Dodd, Mead, 1979.

Earl, Riggins R., Jr. *Dark Symbols, Obscure Signs: God, Self and Community in the Slave Mind.* Maryknoll, N.Y.: Orbis Books, 1993.

Forbes, James A., Jr. "Social Transformation." In *Living with Apocalypse: Spiritual Resources for Social Compassion,* edited by Tilden H. Edwards, 41–60. San Francisco: Harper & Row, 1984.

Foster, Charles R. *The Future of Christian Education: Educating Congregations.* Nashville, Tenn.: Abingdon Press, 1994.

Fox, Matthew. *Original Blessing.* Santa Fe, N.M.: Bear & Co., 1983.

Frazier, E. Franklin. *The Negro Family in the United States.* Chicago: University of Chicago Press, 1939.

Gates, Henry Louis, Jr. "The Face and Voice of Blackness." In *Facing History: The Black Image in American Art, 1740–1940*, edited by Guy C. McElroy, xxix–xlvi. San Francisco: Bedford Arts, 1990.

———. *Loose Canons: Notes on the Culture Wars*. New York: Oxford University Press, 1992.

Geertz, Clifford. *The Interpretation of Cultures*. New York: Basic Books, 1973.

Genovese, Eugene. *Roll, Jordan, Roll: The World the Slaves Made*. New York: Pantheon, 1974.

Grant, Jacquelyn. *White Women's Christ and Black Women's Jesus: Feminist Christology and Womanist Response*. Atlanta: Scholars Press, 1989.

Gutiérrez, Gustavo. *We Drink from Our Own Wells*. Maryknoll, N.Y.: Orbis Books, 1984.

Hale, Janice E. "The Transmission of Faith to Young African American Children." In *The Recovery of the Black Presence: An Interdisciplinary Exploration*, edited by Randall C. Bailey and Jacquelyn Grant, 193–207. Nashville, Tenn.: Abingdon Press, 1995.

Hammarskjöld, Dag. *Markings*. Translated by Leif Sjöberg and W. H. Auden. London: Faber and Faber, 1964.

Hough, Joseph C., Jr., and John B. Cobb Jr. *Christian Identity and Theological Education*. Chico, Calif.: Scholars Press, 1985.

Johnson, James Weldon. *God's Trombones: Seven Negro Sermons in Verse*. New York: Penguin Books, 1976.

Karenga, Maulana. *Introduction to Black Studies*. Los Angeles: Kawaida Publications, 1982.

Kennedy, William B. "The Ideological Captivity of the Non-Poor." In *Pedagogies for the Non-Poor*, edited by Alice F. Evans, Robert A. Evans, and William B. Kennedy, 232–56. Maryknoll, N.Y.: Orbis Books, 1987.

King, Martin Luther, Jr. *Strength to Love*. New York: Harper & Row, 1963.

———. *Stride Toward Freedom: The Montgomery Story*. New York: Harper & Row, 1958.

King, Paul G., Kent Maynard, and David O. Woodyard. *Risking Liberation: Middle Class Powerlessness and Social Heroism*. Atlanta: John Knox Press, 1988.

Kirk-Duggan, Cheryl. "African American Spirituals: Confronting and Exorcising the Evil through Song." In *A Troubling in My Soul: Womanist Perspectives on Evil and Suffering*, edited by Emilie M. Townes, 150–71. Maryknoll, N.Y.: Orbis Books, 1993.

Lincoln, C. Eric. *Coming through the Fire: Surviving Race and Place in America*. Durham: Duke University Press, 1996.

———. *Race, Religion and the Continuing American Dilemma*. New York: Hill & Wang, 1984.

Lincoln, C. Eric, and Lawrence H. Mamiya. *The Black Church in the African American Experience*. Durham, N.C.: Duke University Press, 1990.

Long, Charles H. *Significations: Signs, Symbols, and Images in the Interpretation of Religion*. Philadelphia: Fortress Press, 1986.

Maas, Robin, and Gabriel O'Donnell, eds. *Spiritual Traditions for the Contemporary Church*. Nashville, Tenn.: Abingdon Press, 1990.

Marable, Manning. "The Rhetoric of Racial Harmony." In *America's Original Sin: A Study Guide on White Racism*, edited by Sojourners, 112–16. Washington, D.C.: Editor, 1992.

Mbiti, John S. "African Religion." In *The Study of Spirituality*, edited by Cheslyn Jones, Geoffrey Wainwright, and Edward Yarnold, 513–16. New York: Oxford University Press, 1986.

———. *African Religions and Philosophy*. New York: Praeger, 1969.

———. "Theological Impotence and the Universality of the Church." In *Mission Trends*, edited by Gerald H. Anderson and Thomas F. Stransky, 6–18. New York: Paulist Press, 1976.

McClain, William B. *Come Sunday: The Liturgy of Zion*. Nashville, Tenn.: Abingdon Press, 1990.

McGuire, Meredith. *Religion: The Social Context*. Belmont, Calif.: Wadsworth, 1992.

Mitchell, Henry H. *Black Preaching*. Philadelphia: Lippincott, 1970.

———. *Celebration and Experience in Preaching*. Nashville, Tenn.: Abingdon Press, 1990.

Morris, Calvin S. Interview by authors. Atlanta: Interdenominational Theological Center, 28 June 1996.

Murray, Pauli. "Black Theology and Feminist Theology: A Comparative View." In *Black Theology: A Documentary History, 1966–1979*, edited by Gayraud S. Wilmore and James H. Cone, 398–417. Maryknoll, N.Y.: Orbis Books, 1979.

Neal, Marie Augusta. *The Just Demands of the Poor*. New York: Paulist Press, 1987.

Nouwen, Henri J. M. "Career and Vocation." In *Seeds of Hope: A Henri Nouwen Reader*, edited by Robert Durback, 94–96. New York: Bantam Books, 1989.

———. *Lifesigns: Intimacy, Fecundity, and Ecstacy in Christian Perspective*. New York: Doubleday, 1986.

Opoku, Kofi Asare. "Ancient Wisdom in African Heritage." *International Christian Digest* 4 (May 1988): 34.

———. *West African Traditional Religion*. Jurong, Singapore: FEP International Private Ltd., 1978.

Paris, Peter J. *The Social Teaching of the Black Churches*. Philadelphia: Fortress Press, 1985.

———. *The Spirituality of African Peoples: The Search for a Common Moral Discourse*. Minneapolis: Fortress Press, 1995.

Payne, Wardell J., ed. *Directory of African American Religious Bodies*. Washington, D.C.: Howard University Press, 1995.

Perdue, Charles H., Jr., Thomas E. Barden, and Robert K. Phillips, eds. *Weevils in the Wheat: Interviews with Virginia Ex-Slaves*. Charlottesville: University of Virginia Press, 1994.

Phelps, Jamie. "Black Spirituality." In *Spiritual Traditions for the Contemporary Church*, edited by Robin Maas and Gabriel O'Donnell, 332. Nashville, Tenn.: Abingdon Press, 1990.

Raboteau, Albert J. *Slave Religion: The "Invisible Institution" in the Antebellum South*. New York: Oxford University Press, 1978.

Roberts, Keith. *Religion in Sociological Perspective*. New York: Wadsworth, 1995.

Roberts, J. Deotis. *Liberation and Reconciliation*. Philadelphia: Westminster, 1971.

Rooks, Charles Shelby. *Rainbows and Reality: Selected Writings of the Author*. Atlanta: The ITC Press, 1985.

Runes, Dagobert D., ed. *Dictionary of Philosophy*. Totowa, N.J.: Littlefield, Adams, 1967.

Sarpong, Peter K. "Everyday Tribal Spirituality." *International Christian Digest* 1 (May 1988): 24–26.

Seager, Joni, and Ann Olson. *Women in the World: An International Atlas*. New York: Simon & Schuster, 1986.

Shannon, David T. "'An Ante-bellum Sermon': A Resource for an African American Hermeneutic." In *Stony the Road We Trod: African American Biblical Interpretation*, edited by Cain Hope Felder, 98–123. Minneapolis: Fortress Press, 1991.

Shockley, Grant S. "Black Theology." In *Encyclopedia of Religious Education*, edited by Iris V. Cully and Kendig Brubaker Cully, 80–82. San Francisco: Harper & Row, 1990.

Smith, Theophus H. *Conjuring Culture: Biblical Formulations of Black America*. New York: Oxford University Press, 1994.

———. "The Spirituality of Afro-American Traditions." In *Christian Spirituality: Post Reformation and Modern*, edited by Louis Dupre and Don E. Saliers, 372–414. New York: Crossroad, 1991.

Smith, Wallace Charles. *The Church in the Life of the Black Family.* Valley Forge, Pa.: Judson Press, 1985.

Somé, Malidoma Patrice. *Of Water and the Spirit: Ritual, Magic and Initiation in the Life of an African Shaman.* New York: Penguin Books, 1994.

Songs of Zion. Nashville, Tenn.: Abingdon Press, 1981.

Southern, Eileen. *The Music of Black Americans.* New York: W. W. Norton, 1971.

Spencer, Jon Michael. *Protest and Praise: Sacred Music of Black Religion.* Minneapolis: Fortress Press, 1990.

Stroup, George. "Revelation." In *Christian Theology: An Introduction to Its Traditions and Tasks,* 2nd ed., rev. and enl., edited by Peter C. Hodgson and Robert H. King, 114–40. Philadelphia: Fortress Press, 1985.

Swinton, David H. "The Economic Status of African Americans: 'Permanent' Poverty and Inequality." In *The State of Black America,* edited by Janet Dewart, 25–75. New York: National Urban League, 1991.

Thurman, Howard. *Deep River and the Negro Spiritual Speaks of Life and Death.* Richmond, Ind.: Friends United Press, 1975.

———. *Disciplines of the Spirit.* Richmond, Ind.: Friends United Press, 1987.

———. *For the Inward Journey.* Richmond, Ind.: Friends United Press, 1984.

———. *Meditations of the Heart.* Richmond, Ind.: Friends United Press, 1976.

Tocqueville, Alexis de. *Democracy in America.* Translated by George Lawrence. New York: Doubleday/Anchor Books, 1969.

T'Ofori-Atta, Ndugu G. B. "Eight Stages in the Holistic Life Cycle 'In the Hood' of Traditional African Religion." *Journal of the Interdenominational Theological Center* 23 (Spring 1996): 81–120.

Townes, Emilie M., ed. *A Troubling in My Soul: Womanist Perspective on Evil and Suffering.* New York: Orbis Books, 1993.

Wallis, Jim. *The Soul of Politics: Beyond "Religious Right" and "Secular Left."* New York: Harcourt Brace, 1995.

Washington, James Melvin, ed. *A Testament of Hope: The Essential Writings of Martin Luther King, Jr.* New York: Harper & Row, 1986.

West, Cornel. *Prophecy Deliverance.* Philadelphia: The Westminster Press, 1982.

———. *Race Matters.* Boston: Beacon Press, 1993.

Williams, Cecil, and Rebecca Laird. *No Hiding Place: Empowerment and Recovery for Our Troubled Communities.* New York: Harper-Collins, 1992.

Wilmore, Gayraud. *Black Religion and Black Radicalism.* Maryknoll, N.Y.: Orbis Books, 1983.

———. "Spirituality and Social Transformation as the Vocation of the Black Church." In *Churches in Struggle: Liberation Theologies and Social Change in North America*, edited by William K. Tabb, 240–53. New York: Monthly Review Press, 1986.

Wright, Jeremiah A., Jr. "Unashamedly Black and Unapologetically Christian." In *African Roots: Towards an Afrocentric Christian Witness*, edited by Michael I. N. Dash, L. Rita Dixon, Darius L. Swann, and Ndugu T'Ofori-Atta, 173–202. Lithonia, Ga.: SCP/Third World Literature, 1994.